May 2014

Roger Hilton

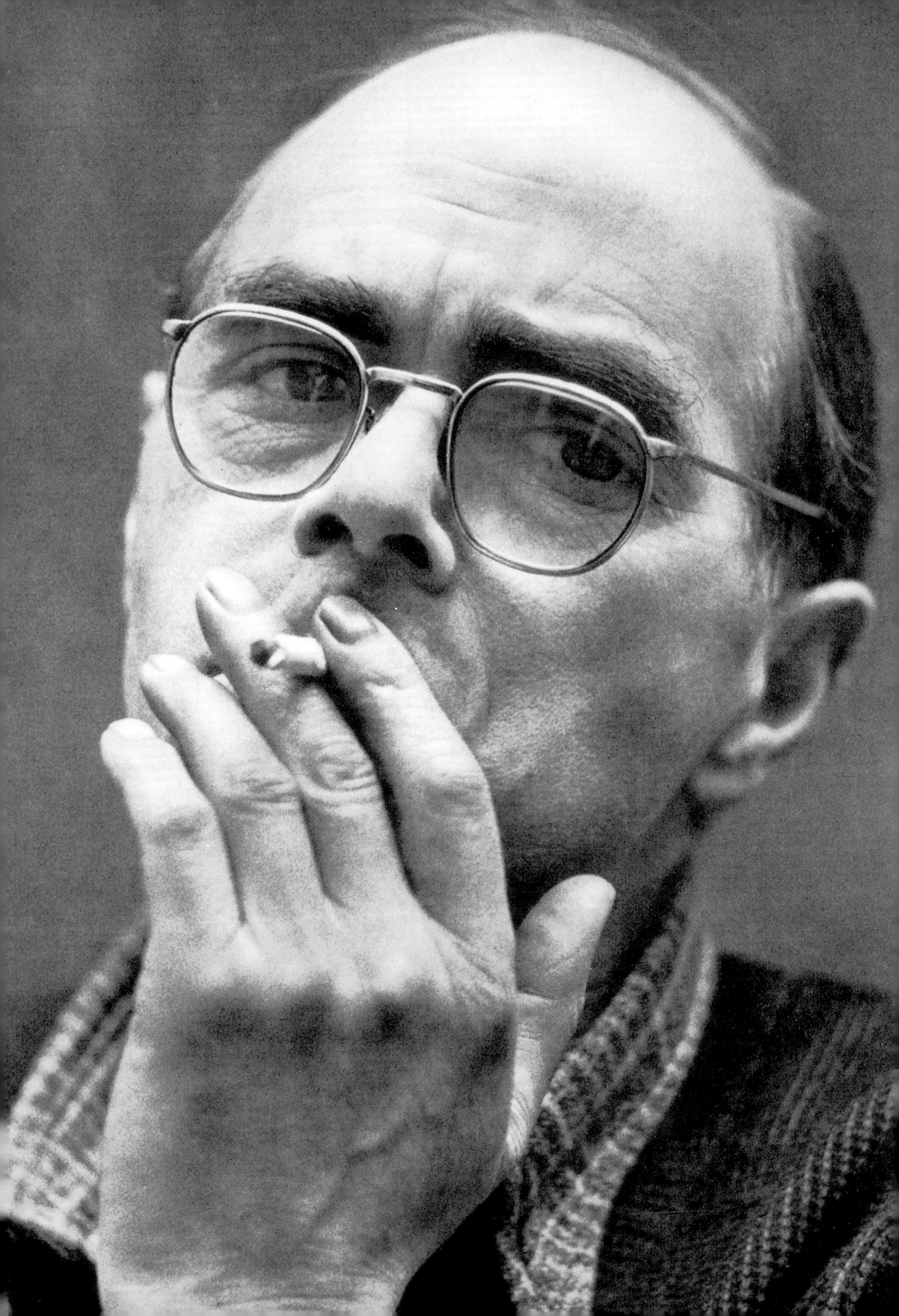

Roger Hilton

Chris Stephens

ST IVES ARTISTS

Tate Publishing

COVER: *July 1953* 1953 (fig.14), detail

BACK COVER: Roger Hilton
Roger Mayne 1956

FRONTISPIECE: Roger Hilton
c.1960

First published 2006 by order of the Tate
Trustees by Tate Publishing, a division of
Tate Enterprises Ltd, Millbank, London SW1P 4RG
www.tate.org.uk/publishing

© Tate 2006

British Library Cataloguing in Publication Data

A catalogue record for this book is available
from the British Library

ISBN-10: 1-85437-669-1

ISBN-13: 978-185437-669-5

Book designed by Caroline Johnston
from a template by Isambard Thomas

Cover concept by Slatter-Anderson, London

Printed in Hong Kong by South Seas
International Press

Measurements are given in centimetres,
height before width

Acknowledgements

I would like to thank Rose Hilton for generous
access to Roger Hilton's archive and for
sharing her memories, thoughts and warmest
hospitality over a long period. Without her help
and kindness this book would have been much
harder and a lot less enjoyable to write. I hope
my debt to previous writers on Hilton's work will
be clear from the text and its notes. Less
specifically, what follows has no doubt been
coloured by conversations over the years with,
among others, Wilhelmina Barns-Graham,
Trevor Bell, Alan Bowness, David Brown,
Michael and Madeline Canney, Ronnie Duncan,
Terry Frost, Stephen Gilbert, Nessie Graham,
Sheila Lanyon, David Lewis, Brian Wall and
Monica Wynter. I should thank all those
collectors and custodians of public collections
who have kindly allowed access to the
paintings and drawings in their care. All at
Jonathan Clark Fine Art have been a help, most
especially Simon Hucker who has fielded
countless requests for assistance with great
patience and efficiency. I am also grateful to
Waddington Galleries, David Archer, John
Austin and Catriona Colledge at Austin/
Desmond Fine Art, Maggie Thornton at the
Redfern Gallery and others who helped find
works by Hilton. At Tate Publishing, Alice
Chasey, Lillian Davies and Sarah Brown have
brought and held it all together. Finally, I thank
Jo and Maria for making it all worthwhile.

St Ives Artists

The light, landscape and working people of
West Cornwall have made it a centre of artistic
activity for over one hundred years. This series
introduces the life and work of artists of
national and international reputation who have
been closely associated with the area and
whose work can be seen at Tate St Ives. Each
author sets out a fresh approach to our
thinking about some of the most fascinating
artistic figures of the twentieth century.

Contents

Introduction

To write on Roger Hilton or, more precisely, to write on his painting, is daunting. It is not surprising that so few have attempted the task. Even one of the most incisive examinations of Hilton's art, by Charles Harrison, begins with the recognition that it is 'difficult'.[1] I was told the story of a young critic who met Hilton in the 1960s and told him that he was to write about him. 'Only a Kafka could write about me,' was the response, 'Or a Dostoyevsky. Or a Hilton.'[2] If that was not warning enough, I then saw Hilton's annotations to another writer's introduction to one of his own exhibitions: 'Lie … wrong … not true … you Courtauld ninny'. It is perhaps appropriate that one approaches writing on Hilton with trepidation as, more than many others, Hilton's paintings make the viewer aware of the transformation that the artist has brought about. They have an apparently natural completeness, but the viewer is still made conscious of the blank canvas that had faced the artist at the outset.

As an art historian, one is often admonished by artists that the works speak for themselves. More than any other, Hilton's paintings seem to fulfil that warning. They are what they are. Their effect on the viewer is immediate and visceral; the response intuitive. It seems indisputable that this stems in large part from the artist's apparently instinctive command of the processes, techniques and materials of painting and drawing. It would appear that his close friend, the painter and critic Patrick Heron, was right when he wrote, 'Roger Hilton is a natural painter.

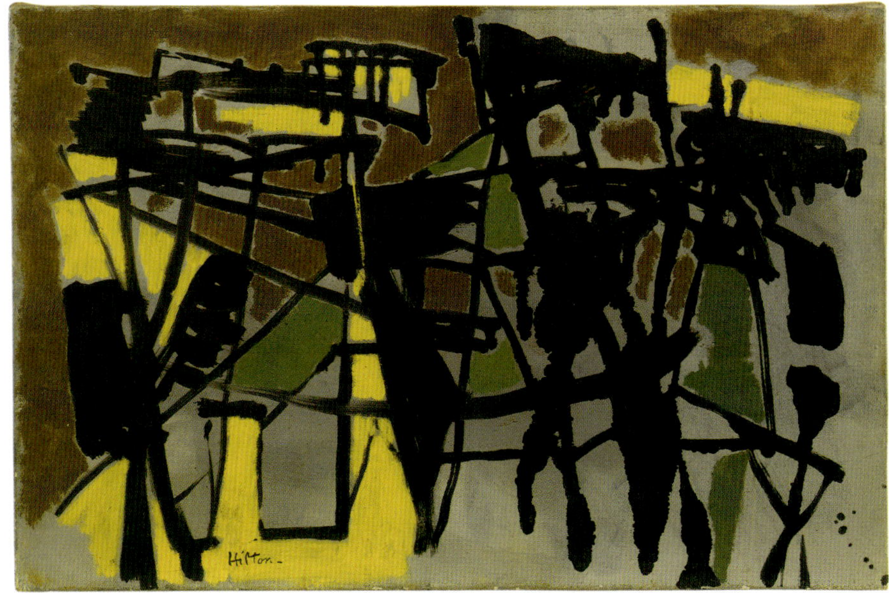

1
Untitled c.1950
Oil on canvas 51 × 76

Private Collection

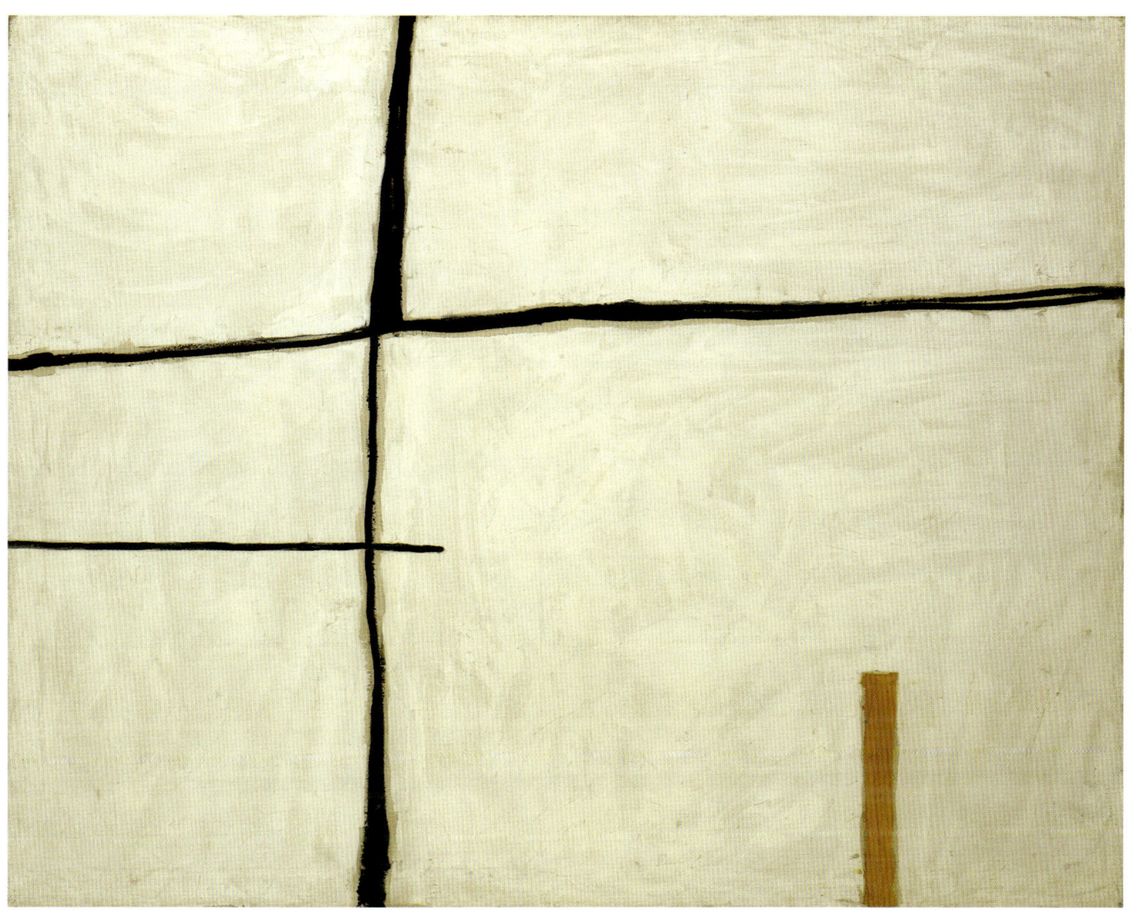

2
Painting 1954 1954
Oil on canvas
101.5 × 127

British Council

That is to say, he cannot put brush to canvas without creating a splotch, smear, streak, stain or smudge (in other words, "a brushstroke") that is charged with expressive quality'.[3] Hilton himself consistently emphasised the importance of an artist's trained command of his medium while insisting that artists 'are born and not made'.[4] Yet, the qualities that Hilton's works possess also stem from his profoundly sophisticated understanding of modernist painting and the historical imperatives that drove it. He combined, that is to say, the idea of painting as an instinctive, natural activity with a theorised view to compare with that of Heron or his American friend and colleague Clement Greenberg. The works are immediately affecting but, in part, gain that quality from an impassioned intellectual position.

It is remarkable how little has been written on Hilton and his art. It is the case that for many years this was true of all his British contemporaries as they continued to be overshadowed and ignored by their American equivalents and their commentators. I do not subscribe to Heron's argument that American Abstract Expressionists and Post-Painterly Abstract painters stole their ideas from the British. It is, however, extraordinary, that an assumption that the progress of art since the Second World War occurred almost exclusively in the United States survives and continues to be promoted. However, over the last decade the literature about this generation of British artists has grown hugely, with books on Heron, Alan Davie, Terry Frost, Peter Lanyon, William Scott, Bryan Wynter and others. Meanwhile, Hilton has received scant attention, though one should

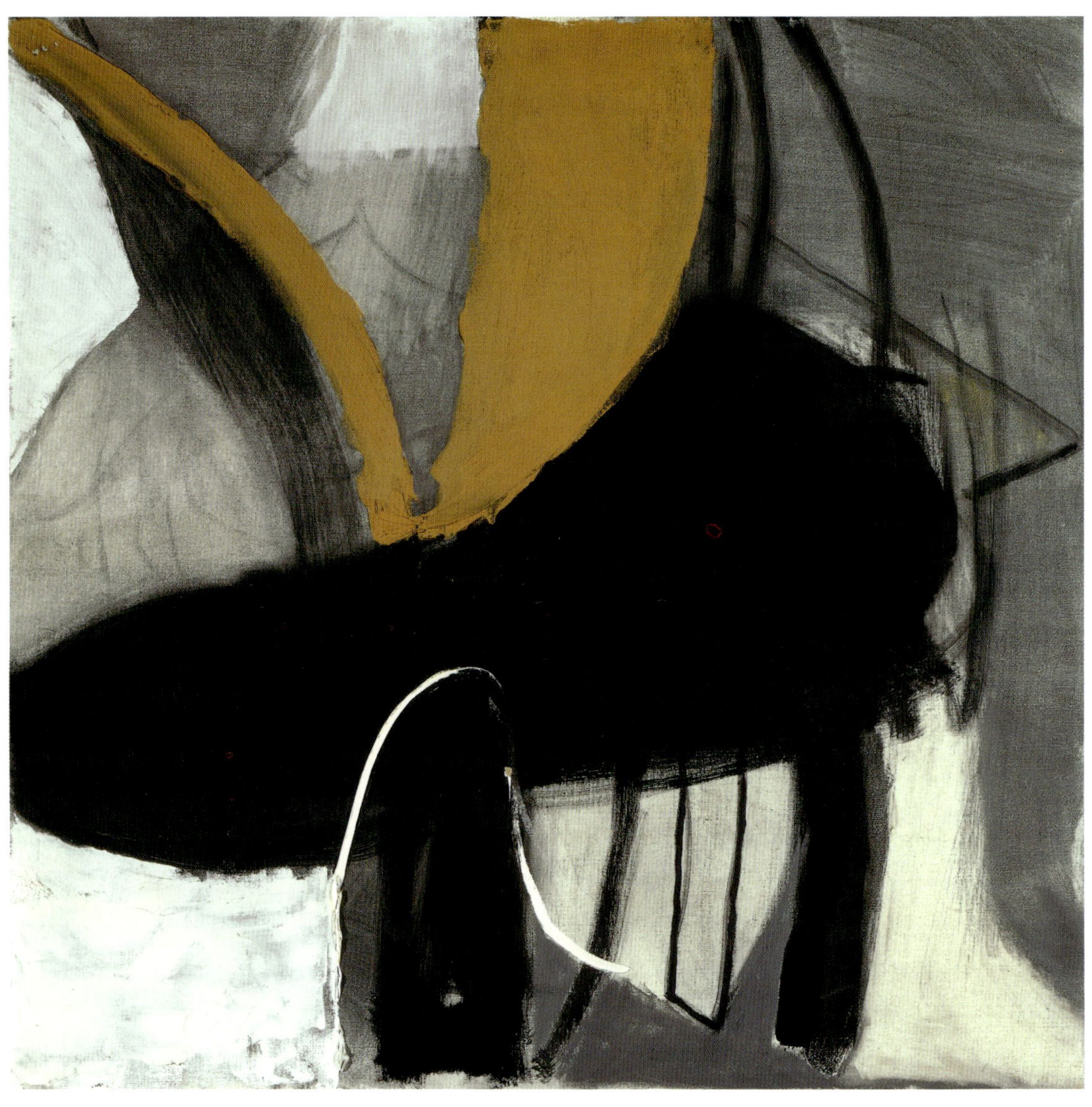

acknowledge the significance of the ground-breaking research conducted by Adrian Lewis into Hilton's life and work and, most especially, into his early years.[5]

As a consequence of this relative neglect, it is hard to gauge what is generally known of Hilton. Such is its prominence that it is probably with St Ives that he is most commonly associated. In fact, he should be seen as semi-detached from that grouping. He did not spend any time among the St Ives artists until 1955, by which time the school was well established, and did not settle permanently in Cornwall until 1965 when it was unquestionably in decline. That said, the issues that Hilton faced in his art were shared with his friends in Cornwall, particularly that of the future of painting and the relationship between abstraction and representation. That artists such as Lanyon and Wynter drew upon landscape or ideas of nature for their work is too often mistakenly ascribed to the unavoidable beauty of their environment. In a similar vein, the appearance of landscape references in Hilton's art in the late 1950s and 1960s has been explained by his visits to Cornwall. In fact, this new departure was part of a wider debate around

3
January 1957 1957
Oil and charcoal on canvas 66 × 66

Tate

4
July 1960 1960
Oil and charcoal on canvas 76.2 × 91.5

Private Collection

abstraction and a return to imagery. If one was to look at their work in terms of painting technique, all of these artists used external visual references – to land-scapes, natural process, bodies or (in the case of William Scott) domestic objects – as a device through which to explore the possibilities of painting. At the same time, we should not ignore the differences between the intentions of these different individuals. While Lanyon, for example, used semi-abstraction to address notions of place and cultural identity, Hilton used it as a means of exploring the erotic and the corporeal. Both, however, used art as a means of exploring the existentialist idea of 'being in the world'.

Hilton struggled with the way forward for painting in the post-war world. The nature of that struggle can be simply summarised as an internal debate between figuration and total non-representation. Before the war, abstract modernism in painting and sculpture had reached a highpoint in the utopian abstraction of such artists as Piet Mondrian and Georges Vantongerloo in Europe and Ben Nicholson and Barbara Hepworth in Britain. An alternative modernist art was represented by the Surrealists who proposed the subconscious, as theorised by Freud, and the irrational as sources for art. In the wake of the war, with the protagonists redistributed around the world, the values that underpinned such developments were subject to review. For a time it was thought that London might be the city to succeed Paris as modernism's capital. At the same time, in continental Europe,

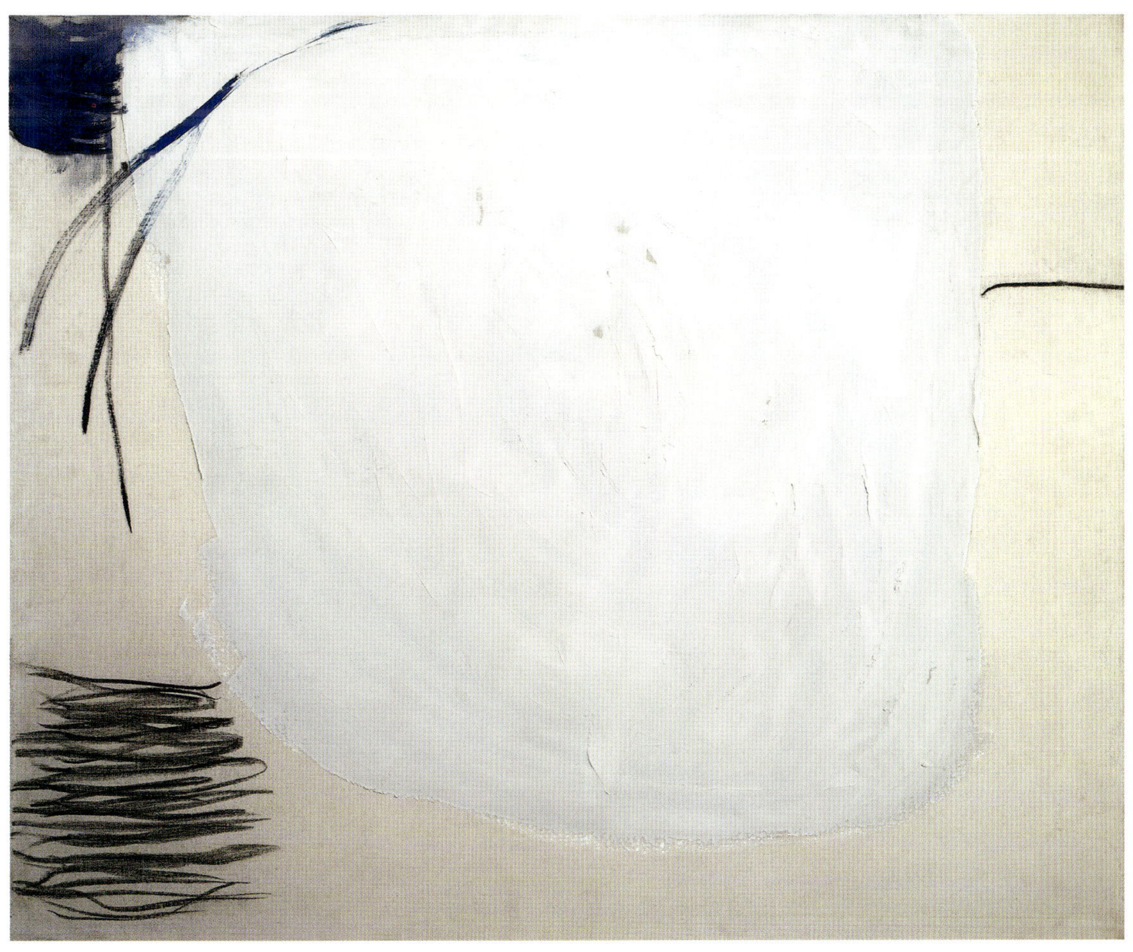

Britain and the United States, artists tested new ways of making painting that spoke to and for this new age. Though the art that emanated from New York would become the benchmark for high modernist practice, Hilton made an important and original contribution to that experimentation.

A series of interrelated writings on art by Hilton survive. They mostly appear to relate to his essay in Lawrence Alloway's *Nine Abstract Artists*, published in 1954.[6] They reveal how he saw art as a conveyor of truths of vital importance to humanity. At the same time, he defined the artist as an existentialist hero. Hilton's optimistic view of painting's role in modern society was clearly derived from that of a generation earlier. He seems to have seen painting as a contributor to a more harmonious existence, particularly in relation to space and architecture. 'The role of a picture has changed considerably', he wrote,

It is no longer regarded as a vehicle for images or even as an arrangement of shapes. It has become an instrument, a kind of catalyst, for the activation of space …We see that their role has become more anonymous and that their effect is not to say 'Look at me' but 'Look at your surroundings'. Ideally they should provoke harmony where none existed before.[7]

In this way, painters are compared by Hilton to philosophers and described as purveyors of universal truths.

Unlike the confidence with which artists such as Nicholson and Mondrian addressed similarly expressed goals, however, Hilton wrote of the solitariness, risk and anxiety imposed upon the artist by such responsibilities. Earlier modernist positioning had been underpinned by different forms of spiritualism. Hilton, however, was avowedly opposed to such beliefs. As his brother would wryly recall,

[Our father] was very strong against alcohol … gambling, irregular sexual activities, swearing and talk of the paranormal. (Roger agreed on the last point.)[8]

So these universal truths would pertain to humankind's position in common existence rather than an ideal, higher reality. He was not referring, however, to what he saw as the banal details that realist painters depicted in their work. Hilton saw art as a means by which people might be made aware of larger, worldly realities. 'The painter today is like the ancient alchemist', he wrote. 'He is concerned not so much with visible reality as with reality *tout court*.'[9] This reality could be universal, and art an 'act of faith', but that did not mean Hilton was a political idealist anymore than he was a spiritualist.

It is not the artist's business to be a social worker. He is an explorer of reality, of the consciousness of man and of his relations to the Universe … Art should be an immediate act of affirmation. Its message should be faith. Faith, not in a world where all men are equal, but faith in an ultimate truth beyond the present flux … It is self-evident that in a universal state, where peace and harmony reigned and where all men were equal, the need for art would be even greater than now. The condition of men would be worse, having no cause or no grip upon their situation on the spinning globe … The confrontation with a work of art has been called the experience of beauty; I would prefer to call it the experience of reality.[10]

Thus, he dismissed political extremism as succinctly as he did religion and suggested the lack of idealistic goals was a good thing and utopia an unhappy, unnatural state. Twenty years later he would reaffirm that 'every true artist is a revolutionary but only in his own domain. He probably doesn't even vote'.[11]

To seek and to try to articulate fundamental truths was an ordeal for the artist. Like the shaman that in Hilton's view they resemble, painters suffer for their talent and the responsibility that comes with it. In this view, the artist must dig deep to find the universal truths in a world without God and without hope of equality.

5

January 1962 1962
Oil on canvas 114 × 127

Ulster Museum, Belfast

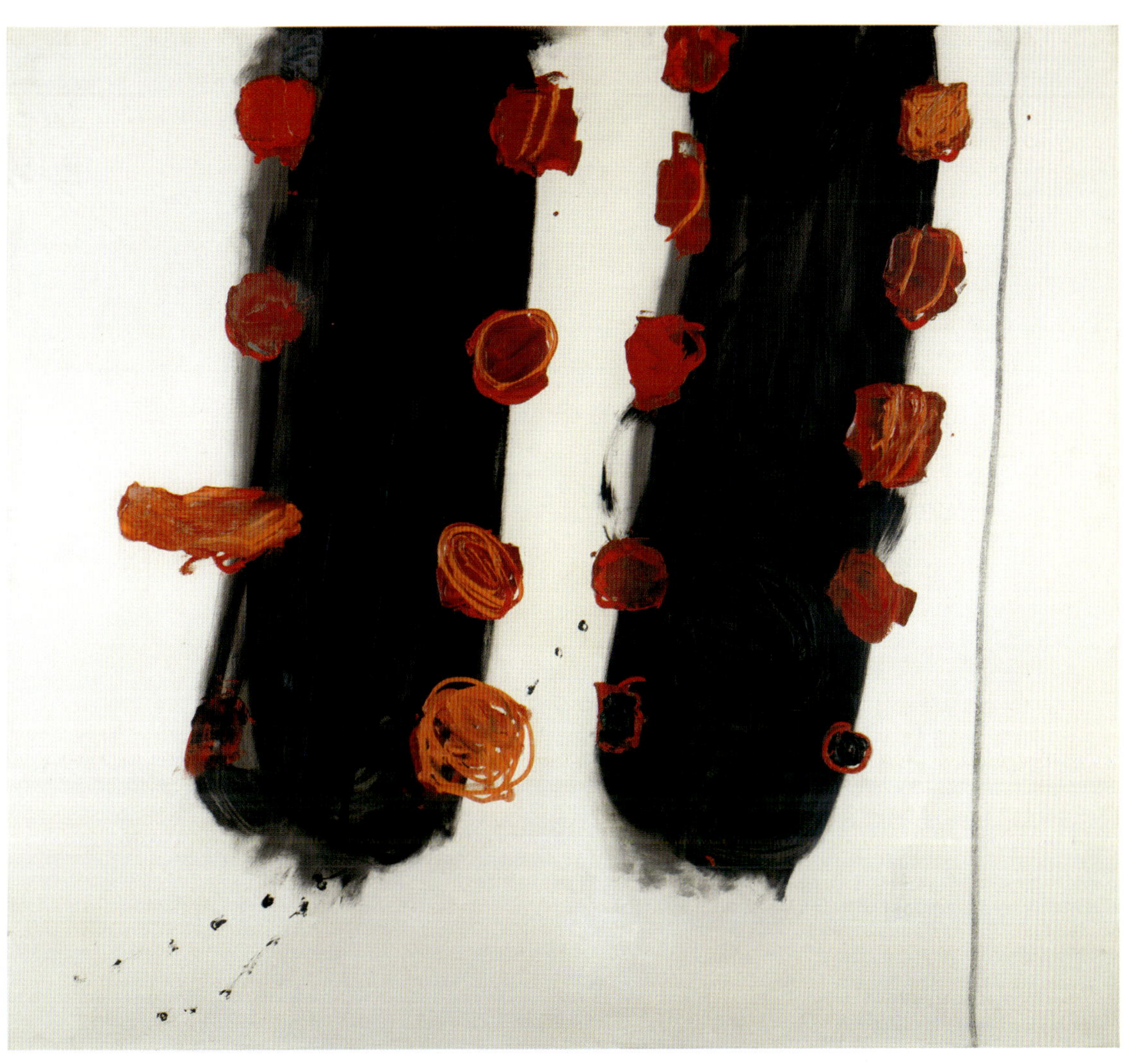

Consequently, 'The painting is the visible record of the scars left by a battle which takes place in the hinterland of [the artist's] being'.[12] Hilton's position is consistent with the philosophy of existentialism which was prevalent in post-war Europe and America and which he had encountered in Paris in the 1930s. Thus he combined a faith in abstraction with a philosophical position more commonly associated with such figurative artists as Francis Bacon and Alberto Giacometti, whose work more obviously addresses the theme of the human condition. Perhaps the closest parallel for Hilton's fusion of a modernist paring down of his art with an acceptance of humankind's ultimate hopelessness and absurdity is the writing of Samuel Beckett. It is appropriate that one of Hilton's most important friendships should be with someone whose work is comparable to that of Beckett, the poet W.S. Graham. Graham wrote of the artist maiming themselves for the job. In a similar vein, Hilton wrote: 'there is no difference between painters and any other creative individual — they are all conducting a life and death struggle with *existence* … The artist, like the priest or philosopher, tries to make sense out of the whole bloody whirligig'.[13] Such a statement could seem facetious if it had not been made by someone who had direct experience of life and death struggles.

Hilton belonged to a generation of artists whose careers were interrupted by the Second World War. For that reason, he was slow to reach a mature style. One might see him having two periods of apprenticeship: one in Paris during the 1930s, interwoven with two brief periods at the Slade School of Art in London, and the second during the years immediately following the war. It was therefore only in his early forties that Hilton arrived at a distinctive and coherent style and position with the austere paintings of 1953–4. At that point he abandoned a style similar to that of such Parisian artists as Alfred Manessier for a stark manner of interlocking blocks of solid colour. This was the type of work he was making while formulating his theory of art as the vehicle for a universal truth. Even in these apparently most abstract of works, references to the human body can be discerned and it is just that aspect that would dominate Hilton's deliberations over the future of painting. This book will document how, gradually, he dealt with the relationship between painting, drawing, the body and the erotic. We will see his work pass from these austere abstracts of 1953–4, through a more complex and more heavily painted style in which figures seem more regularly to be implied, to a distinctive manner in which oil paint and charcoal line combine in the most unorthodox way to allude to the body and its functions. During the 1960s, the suggested bodies finally emerged overtly as Hilton adopted unashamedly a fully figurative mode of representation. The final chapter deals with the works in gouache, made in his sick bed, which were both a departure from and a continuation of this slowly emergent figuration.

A key aim of this book is to track Hilton's progressive exploration of the boundaries between figuration and abstraction. Hilton's investigation was part of a sophisticated progression of modernist painting and of the notion of an avant-garde. All of this sounds terribly earnest and there is no doubt that Hilton viewed his work with great seriousness. However, it is important to recognise the degree to which one can see his character informing the work. Interviews with the artist and the personal recollections of others reveal a man of great intelligence and wit, ruthless and perceptive in his criticism and interrogation of others (and himself), aggressive and loving, acerbic and waspish in his humour. These qualities can be seen to be among the elements that determined the character of Hilton's art. We would be wrong to elevate the theoretical or aesthetic sides at the expense of the human and instinctive.

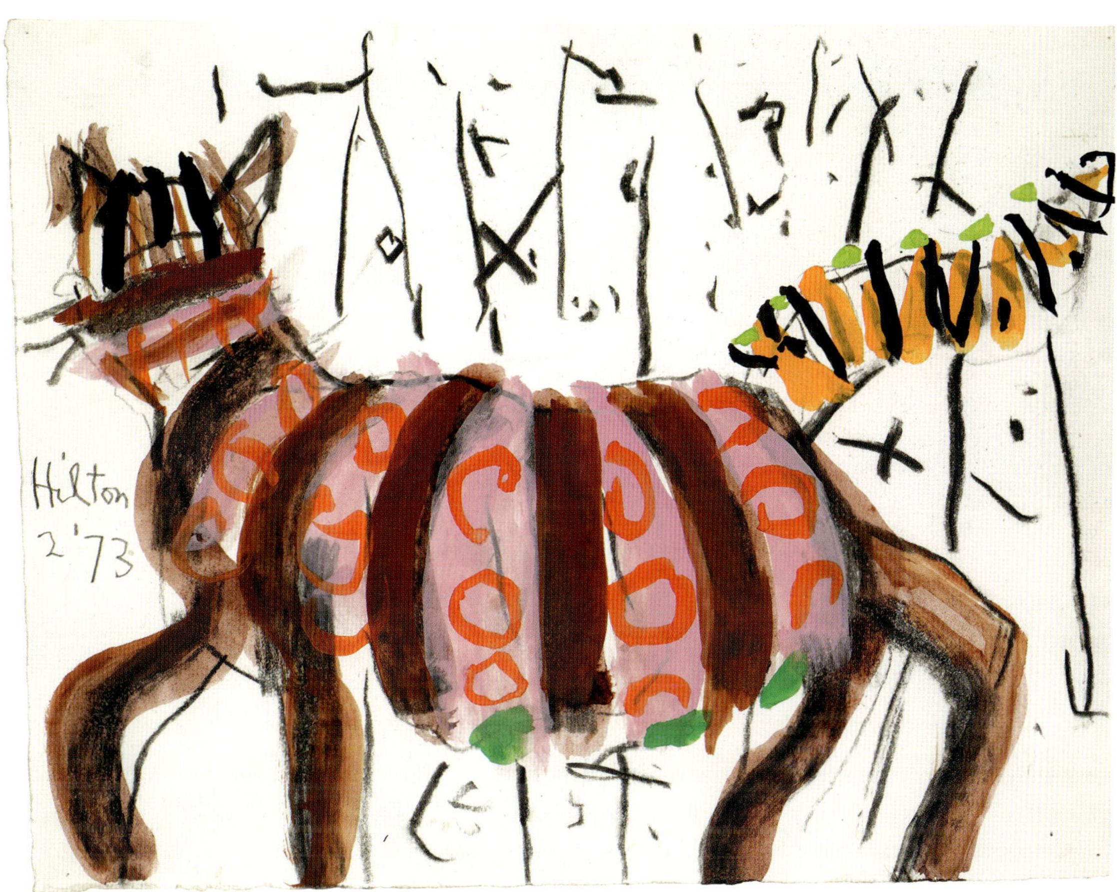

6
Untitled 1973
Gouache on paper
28 × 35.5

The British Museum

One should say, however, that hitherto Hilton's work has been overshadowed to an unfortunate degree by his personal circumstances, specifically his alcoholism. It is true that his addiction had a fundamental effect on his career. This is most clearly demonstrated by the huge body of late works (discussed in the final chapter) that in part owes its existence to the fact that the artist was bedridden as a result of his drinking. It is also the case that he did little to disguise his condition. Indeed, at times he appeared to vaunt it. His state of health in the last few years became part of the mythology of modern British art history through photographs and, most famously, his interview and letter published in *Studio International* in March 1974. There were precedents earlier in his career: in November 1963 the press was full of photographs of Hilton aiming a kick at his own work – *March 1963* – which had just won the John Moores Prize. Without reinforcing romantic notions about artists and addiction, one can recognise an important relationship between Hilton, his work, his alcoholism and his view of the artist as existential hero. At the same time, one must assert the fact that the nature of all of Hilton's work was the result of conscious and deliberate decisions by the artist.

1
1911–1952

Roger Hilton would vehemently deny that he was late to arrive at a mature style. When Alan Bowness wrote that his had been 'an extremely long and slow development' and that 'no recognition came to him until he was well into his forties', Hilton's annotated reply was clear:

You have only just appeared on the scene Mr Bowness preceded by Anthony Blunt. Pete Piper Blunt incidentally reviewed my 1936 show in the New Statesman. So much for your slow developer. … My first one man show was 1936 with a brilliant large oil of my sister. I only wish I had it. The development on the contrary was v. rapid apart from occasional sessions at the ABC factory Camden Town & the Continental Exchange.[1]

Nevertheless, one should dare to say that Bowness was right. It was only at the beginning of the 1950s that Hilton began to work in a style that might be associated with the avant-garde and, even then, it was conspicuously derivative of other artists such as Manessier and William Gear. Even the austere paintings of 1953–4, which are the first works in which a distinctive Hilton voice might be heard, are clearly heavily indebted to others. It is not unreasonable to say he reached artistic maturity in his early forties which, given his untimely death just short of his sixty-fourth birthday, makes his career extremely short.

Despite all that, considerable interest has been shown in Hilton's early years. The art historian Adrian Lewis has pieced together his movements and developments from childhood to middle age. More importantly, Hilton himself, as the quotation above suggests, considered his early work important. He ensured examples of his pre-war painting were included in his retrospective at the Serpentine Gallery, London, in 1974, for example. Even to his last days he would refer, directly or not, to his training in pre-war Paris. He believed in an artist's innate talent, so it is consistent that he sought to identify early demonstrations of such proficiency. There is, nevertheless, little in his pre-war work, however competent, to suggest the sophistication with which he would be able to revise modern painting in the 1950s.

What then, one might ask, is to be learnt from an examination of his years of development? Hilton would place great emphasis on technical knowledge, seeing successful art as a coming together of technique and a quasi-mystical idea of the search 'for the philosopher's stone'. More prosaically, one might say, as Bowness suggested, that the reason the mature Hilton could paint with such fluency and authority was the long years of study and practice. It was in Hilton's earlier life that he acquired technical knowledge and perhaps aesthetic values, but this period may also offer some clues to his broader development. To enquire into the causes for his inner conflicts and personal demons is not simply prurient, as among them one might also find causes for his continual questioning of his art and the value and direction of it.

The strange combination of conservatism and artistic non-conformism that could be discerned in Roger Hilton might be traced to his family. His father, Oscar, was a doctor and his mother, Louisa (Sampson), had trained at the Slade School of Art. The family name had been Hildesheim but, though the family had been resident in Britain since the mid-nineteenth century, they changed to Hilton in 1916 in response to prevalent anti-German feeling. Roger was the second of four siblings (he had two brothers and a sister to whom he remained close). His mother's diary records his liveliness and early artistic leanings. It is perhaps telling that she not only clearly encouraged his creativity but that so many of his childhood drawings survive.

Hilton attended a Montessori school from the age of five to seven and later went to Bishops Stortford College when he failed to get into Marlborough College, the public school attended by both his brothers. The influence of both parents is, presumably, reflected in the fact that he became torn between his original intention to pursue a career as a doctor and his desire to study art. He accepted plans for him to study medicine at Oxford. However, in April 1929 he failed to win a place at Oriel College and, though enquiring about other colleges, had already been interviewed for the Slade School of Art. His mother recorded that, after he had visited Henry Tonks at the Slade to get an objective judgement of his potential,

I asked him how he would be feeling tonight if Mr Tonks had given a favourable opinion. He said he would be feeling overjoyed and with no regrets for the lost university life … Roger and Oscar and I have had an exhausting evening – Doctor versus Artist.[2]

It seems his mother's tacit encouragement of his art came to the fore and Hilton started at the Slade School in London's Bloomsbury in October 1929.

In the 1920s and 1930s, the Slade was a conservative institution protecting traditional values of drawing and painting. The leading teachers had been there since the late nineteenth century, including the professor Henry Tonks, famed for his teaching of old master drawing technique, and Philip Wilson Steer. Shortly before he retired, Tonks noted that he believed Hilton 'has something in him … I cannot make any forecast as to the future, but at least he has a chance, he is just one of those who *might* come to something'.[3]

The sentiment appears not to have been mutual, as Hilton declined a scholarship in 1931 and elected to go to Paris.

'Roger wants to get right away from us all here. Four years right away. Paris probably and we stop expecting things from him', his mother noted on 2 June 1931. The pressure of family expectation and the anxiety of disappointing seems to have become common as Hilton grew up. It was certainly the case that his painting had developed in a direction that did not please his mother. She thought all but one of the works he brought back from a trip to Dorset in 1931 as 'very poor', and wrote to him,

that thing you did in Devonshire of the cat and shapes of colour – also boned woman – make me sick. You are wandering about at present in body and mind … you are suffering from your reading and your ideas, all in advance of your execution … I think too much reading of the lives of the modern painters is not very good for someone following their trade … The long-haired, unshaven, morose, inconsiderate and selfish young man has temporarily ousted the Roger whom one catches glimpses of every hour … The real Roger is still a great dear – with a cracking laugh, rather a dude and interested in everything.[4]

Hilton was aged nineteen years old. He wished to break away from his parents, settle in Paris, explore new forms of picture making, and he was infatuated with

Guilhen Perrier, a friend of his brother's future wife. He was, one might say, the quintessential young artist driven by a creative spirit of exploration and libidinous desire.

In later life, Hilton would say that he spent most of the 1930s in Paris. In fact, he probably spent little more than a total of two years there. Lewis has pointed out that while chronologies presumably approved by the artist stated that Hilton attended the Académie Ranson in Paris, under Roger Bissière, from 1931 to 1939, Bissière's testimonial for Hilton was written in July 1935 and stated that he had attended for ten months only. In claiming a greater Parisian apprenticeship than was the case, Hilton implicitly laid claim to a certain modernist lineage and to a particular taste, as reflected both in his insistence on painting values he learnt there and on French taste in food and other of life's sensual pleasures.

If the Slade had focused on Tonks's teaching of traditional drawing skills, Bissière concentrated on painting. Hilton's sister-in-law, who also studied at the Académie Ranson, could not recall the master 'ever criticising the *drawing* in a painting … What he was most insistent on was colour against colour, and change of tone … Another law of Bissière's was never change colour without changing tone'.[5] Hilton would repeat this mantra in notes written for his wife thirty years later. As a distinctive range of colours and confident command of the effects of their combinations would become one of the key characteristics of Hilton's mature work, this lesson seems to have been of crucial importance. It certainly seemed so to the artist at the time, as he wrote to his parents of Bissière:

I know his main ideas already. Simplification and correct colour values … this attention to 'valeurs' is what I need and will perhaps stop my painting looking like dead fish … I have no need to be taught anything about plastic values.[6]

He reiterated the importance of simplification a couple of weeks later, writing: 'The point is a few right colours instead of a hundred and one wrong ones'.[7]

Hilton shuttled between Paris and England, occupying various studios in the French capital, sharing flats in London and staying at the family's cottage at Litton Cheney, Dorset. His art was, one might surmise, similarly various. Judging by his mother's critique, his work had started to show the impact of modernist painting before he left for Paris. In the summer of 1932, he was reported to be making 'abstract' paintings and landscapes. Images of a considerable number of Hilton's paintings of the 1930s have been gathered and none seems fully abstract. While there are some landscapes, the large majority are figurative and almost all are of the nude or partially nude female form. In most cases attention is thrown onto the body through the lack of any detailed context: in some works the figure occupies a post-Cubist space of hatched and inter-locking planes; in others, she stands or reclines in the most minimal suggestion of a landscape. It is not only the frequency of the standing nude and the reclining odalisque that brings Matisse to mind as, often, Hilton's line recalls the master's work of the 1910s. The Cubist planes were a characteristic of Bissière's own painting but it seems clear from the surviving images that as well as the classes at the Académie Ranson – and also at the Atelier Colorossi – Hilton was paying close attention to Matisse and Picasso. Like those artists and their followers he was interested in the art of other cultures. His friend Michael Stewart recalled Hilton being for a time interested in Coptic art and the influence of Romano-Egyptian painting might be seen in the portrait of the object of Hilton's unrequited love – Guilhen Perrier – that the artist himself described as 'from my Byzantine phase' (see fig.7).[8]

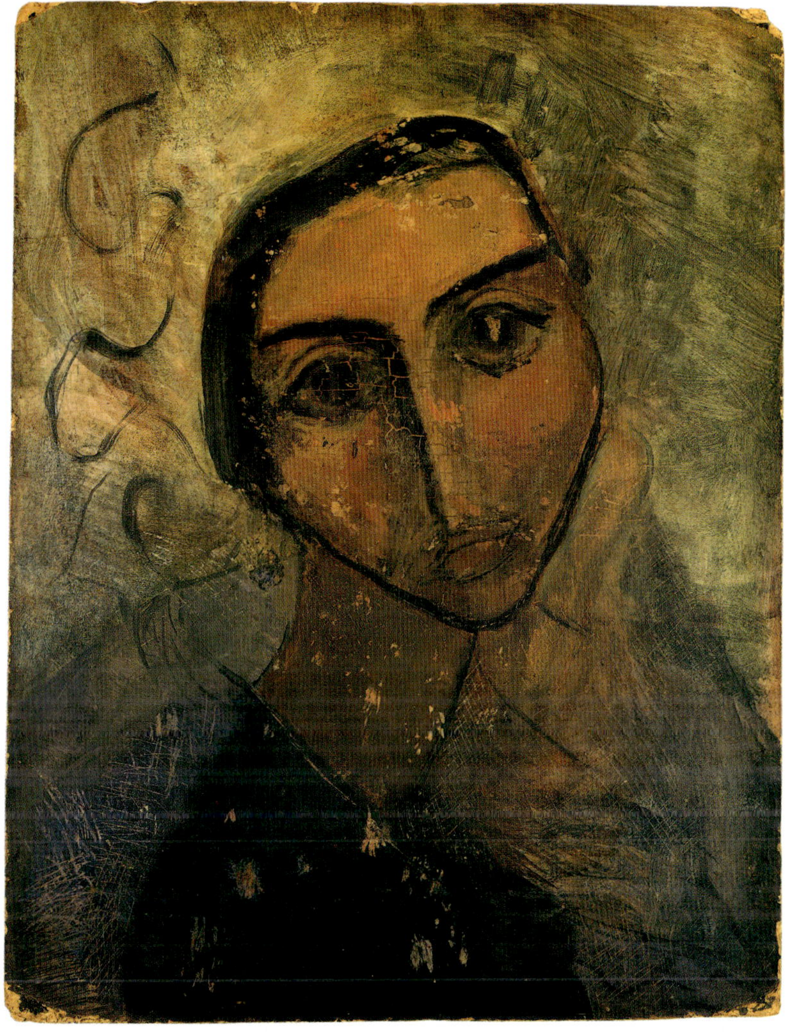

7
Portrait of Guilhen
c.1932
Oil on board
52.7 × 40.6
Private Collection

With his cross-Channel shuttling and changeable manners of painting, Hilton's career before the war can seem somewhat haphazard. It is likely that this is exaggerated by our incomplete knowledge of his movements and activities and, more importantly, our uncertainty about the dates of many works. In any case, his career was developing. He attended some classes at the Royal Academy in London and returned briefly to the Slade (1934–5) in order to get his diploma so that he would be able to teach. His first public showing seems to have been at the Wertheim Gallery in early 1933 as one of 'the Twenties Group', a collection of artists under thirty. He showed again at the Cooling Gallery and his work was accepted by the Bloomsbury-dominated London Group in 1935, 1936 and 1938, though his application for membership was turned down. He had his first one-person exhibition at the Bloomsbury Gallery in January 1936, which received a rather qualified review from Anthony Blunt, then an advocate of realism in art, who was a friend of Hilton's brother. The critic commented on Hilton's 'tendency to a dry method of composition and to give full play to an unusual feeling for restrained and delicate colour-harmonies and to a considerable ability in a rather swaggering use of paint'.[9] Bloomsbury was not put off, as Vanessa Bell and

Duncan Grant visited Hilton in Paris in May 1937 and selected *Seated Model* (fig.8) for Agnew's Coronation Exhibition that summer.

Whatever progress Hilton's career was making, the outbreak of war put paid to it. Like other artists of his generation, the course of Hilton's career was shaped by the interruption. Though to what degree one can only speculate, it seems unimaginable that such a profound and different experience would not have wrought a huge change on his mental attitude and, therefore, on the art he subsequently produced. In any event, Hilton's war and his attitude to it are both telling of the man. He enlisted as soon as war was declared in September 1939. He was clearly impatient and, volunteering 'for a dangerous job', joined the Commandos soon after they were established in June 1940. Paris was occupied by German forces that same month. As a commando, Hilton was sure to see dangerous situations, but did not shirk from them. On the contrary, one colleague remembered an extraordinary act of bravery. During a raid on the Norwegian port of South Vaagso, Hilton was sent on an apparently fatal mission to fetch ammunition. Several others had died or got lost in the attempt but Hilton returned laden with grenades and, when asked how he managed it, explained that he had walked down the main street in clear sight of the enemy. Some would see it as a sign of naivety as well as courage.

Hilton was less fortunate during the disastrous raid on Dieppe on 18–19 August 1942. By the end of that month he had been reported missing and his parents learnt on 24 September that he was a Prisoner of War. His correspondence suggested that he enjoyed the enforced idleness of the prison. A few months earlier he had reflected on his own character:

I am a monomaniac of some sort, I think. Crazy. Incapable of fitting in or taking part or whatever the rest of humanity does. ... I like being selfish and lazy. I am not by any means wholly bad. I have a streak of nobility and generosity somewhere ... I am still regrettably submerged in a private world and with no strong sense of reality. When I get into 'serious' positions like this, where we are training to hold positions of responsibility, my inclination is to do something completely daft ... I am a vagabond at heart ... I am sorry I am not a more satisfactory sort of son.[10]

Whatever the conditions of his imprisonment, as German defeat drew near he and his fellow prisoners were forced to march hundreds of miles from Silesia in southern Poland to Bavaria in the heart of Germany. Ruth Hilton, whom Roger had met shortly before the war and whom he married in 1947, recalled his descriptions of the event:

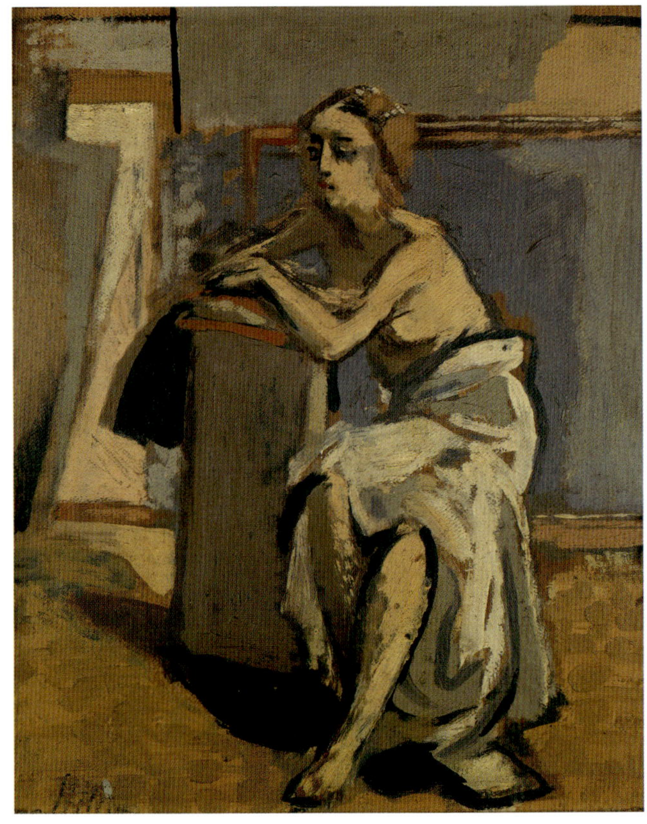

8
Seated Model 1934–5
Oil on board
34.3 × 26.7
Private Collection

9
Brown Standing Form
c.1947–9
Oil on canvas
45.7 × 38.1
Private Collection

What began as an orderly retreat became an every-man-for-himself rout as those amazing months went past. He didn't talk much about it, but I feel certain he was not concealing some fearful experience. He was not upset by fearful experiences, didn't worry about physical hardship, and was extremely brave – a sort of ridiculous bravado sometimes – in the face of danger. Many died of hunger, cold or the brutality of the guards. 'I was always a good walker', he once said to me.[11]

Nevertheless, when Hilton in later life drafted cursory notes for a biographical chronology he suggested a more profound effect:

War. Army (second school). Manual work. Horror. Death. Plains in snow.
On return, life seen as gratuitous gift.[12]

Even before he was captured, he had suggested in a letter to his parents how the experience of war was affecting his outlook on the world. 'I can see nothing but killing and slaughter and dead bodies on the one hand and these ordered lives on the other. This is the thing which is eating my soul and spirit'.[13] Of course, it is hard not to make the connection, as others have, between these experiences and Hilton's self-destruction through addiction. Perhaps one can speculate with a little more security that the events of war which Hilton saw more directly than many demonstrated the inherent brutality and randomness of life that underpin the existential attitude that clearly informed his view of art and the work of the artist in the years that followed.

Whatever the effect of his wartime experiences on his psychological condition and philosophical position, it did nothing for his art. What we know of his painting of the years following the war shows Hilton to be directionless and, apparently, lacking imaginative ideas. What survives of his work of these years is difficult to date and one cannot be certain that it is the best. Ironically, perhaps, his life showed a greater tendency to order. He married Ruth David, a violinist,

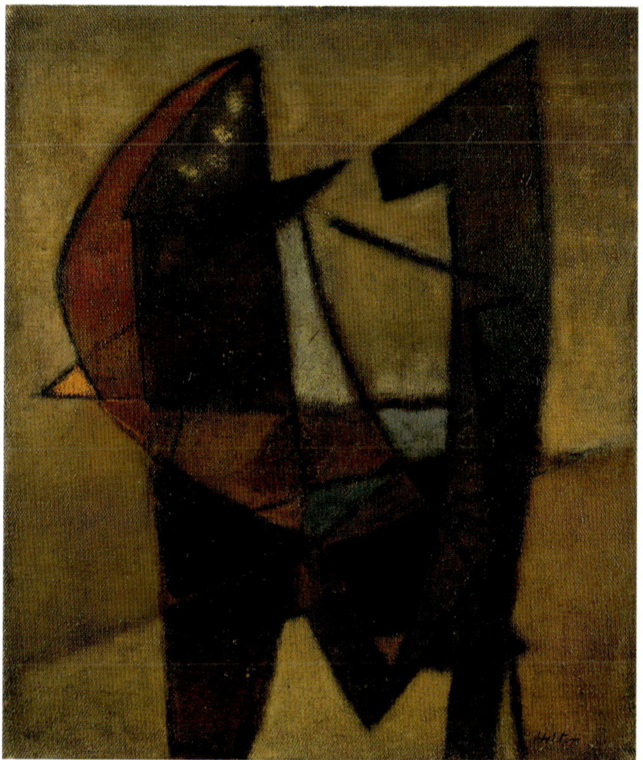

in June 1947 and their first child, Matthew, was born in August the next year. He made occasional visits to Paris and continued to be shown in the odd group exhibition. Times were not easy, however, and Hilton taught in several secondary schools and even worked at the Continental Telephone Exchange. Ruth recalled that in 1949 she had taken a number of paintings to Paris and several galleries showed them, including the prestigious Galerie Maeght. Nevertheless, and despite the growing success of his contemporaries, Hilton insisted his painting was 'not good enough yet'. At the time their second child, Rose, was born in 1950 he complained: 'Painting is hell – I don't want it'.[14]

It was around this time that a major turning point came when Hilton determined to abandon representation and to engage with avant-garde aesthetics. His interest in

Picasso had already, it would seem, drawn him close to non-figuration. While his pre-war paintings revealed his appreciation of Picasso's more classicising works, the post-war *Brown Standing Form* (fig.9) seems to draw upon the more violent imagery as seen, most famously, in Picasso's *Guernica*. Hilton showed alongside three other artists at the Artists International Association gallery in August 1950. The titles of the works suggest they were figurative but it is hard to judge their nature or the degree of their abstraction. One critic recorded that they demonstrated 'the current Parisian idiom − harsh and acrid' − and a knowledge of Francis Bacon.[15] Both might be consistent with a Picasso-esque style.

At the end of the 1940s, however, Hilton produced a number of works in a style Patrick Heron usefully described as 'impressionist' because of its 'broken surfaces'.[16] In these works, soft-edged areas of colour interleave with a framework, usually black, irregular in form and structural, like the armature of a sculpture. Heron's brief description captures the essential qualities of these paintings: 'the broken surface with its fuzzy, impressionist vibration of brushed smudges, some stringy and tenuous, others fat and rotund, soft blobs of colour'.[17] In some the predominance of the black framework and the richness of the other colours gives the work a brooding darkness. Others are lighter, as softer colours are slotted into the forms produced by the interlocking linear structure. Looking back a few years later, the critic Lawrence Alloway remembered that Hilton's work of that time developed from 'a sensuous disorder' in which 'light glowed and ripe fruit splashed in an over-grown Klee garden' into 'a sombre tonal range in which patches of rich colour were embedded in black chiaroscuro, with strong emotive connotations'.[18]

These paintings were unmistakably Parisian, reflecting the influence of one aspect of the movement that would become known as *tachisme*. The term derives from the French for brushmark − *tache* − and indicates a form of painting in which the individual gesture is given primary importance. Before the term *tachisme* was coined in 1951, the more suggestive 'lyrical abstraction' had been employed.[19] Hilton had maintained contact with artistic developments in Paris, though the impact of the Occupation had brought into question its status as the art capital of the world. Hilton later told Heron that the change in his work came about in part as a result of his acquaintance with Alfred Manessier and William Gear, a Scot living in Paris. Both artists employed black frameworks in their abstract compositions, though Gear's tended to be heavier, more architec-

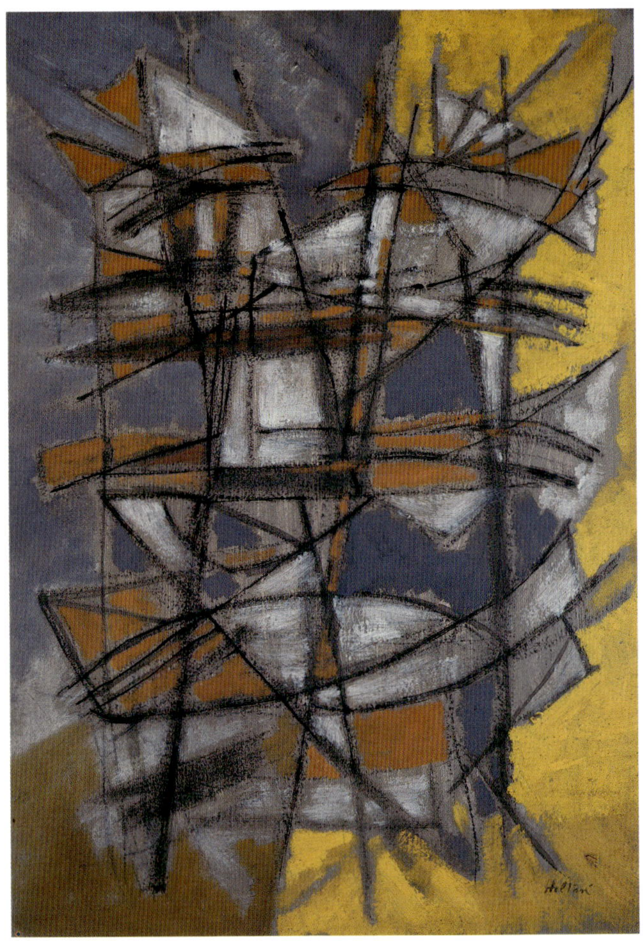

10
Composition with Yellow c.1950
Oil on canvas
53.4 × 38.1
Ronnie Duncan Collection

11
Composition c.1950−2
Oil on canvas
66 × 55.9
Private Collection

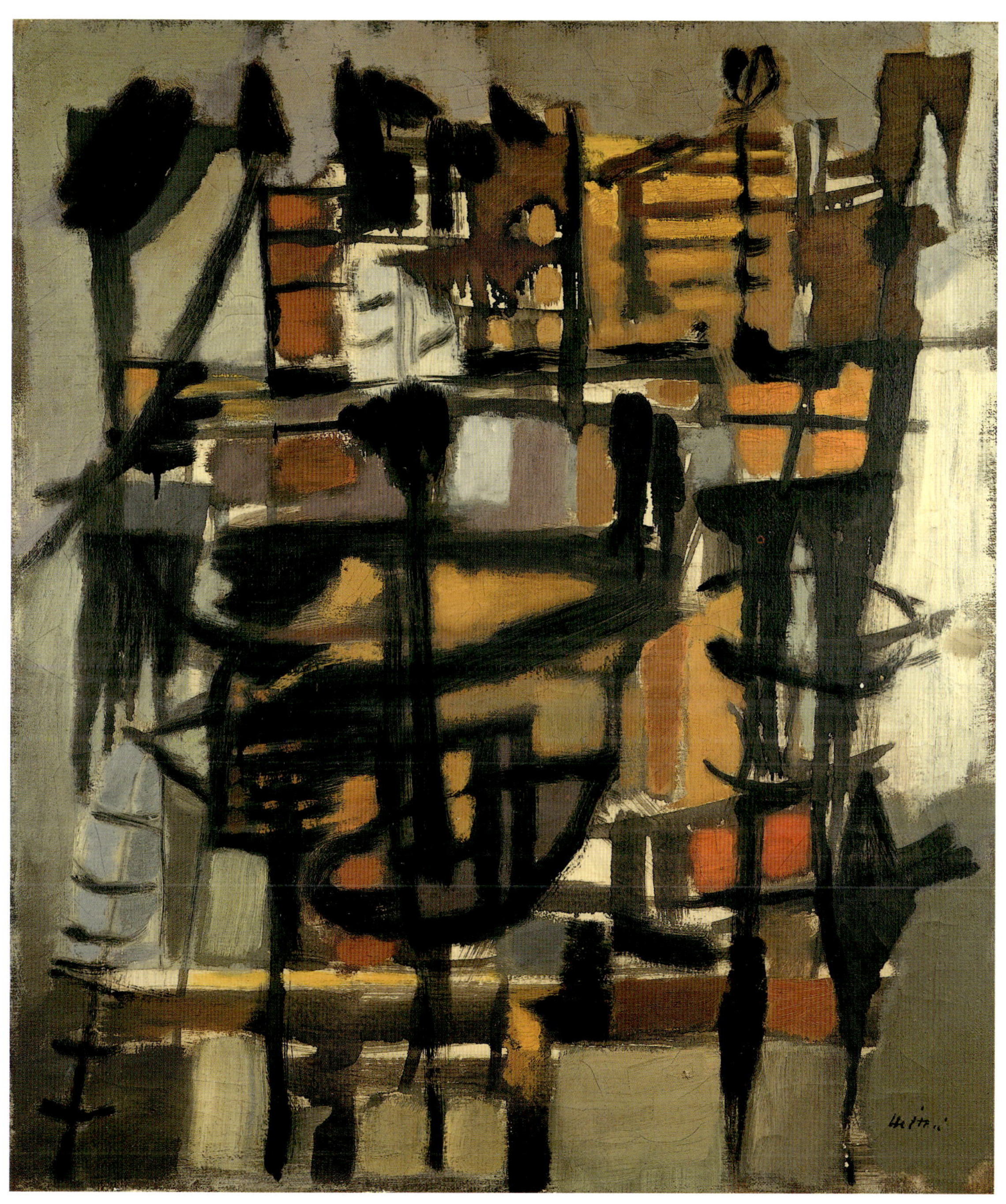

tonic and to retain occasional allusions to objects or landscape. His compositions were initially very centred, as if he were depicting a free-standing abstract construction, but around 1950 they began to reach out to the edges of the frame, providing a more all-over compositional effect. The same phenomenon can be discerned in Hilton's work. The structure of Hilton's paintings varies. Some works appear rectilinear and rigid, akin to some of Gear's. In others, such as *Composition c.*1950–2 (fig.11), there is greater sense of the movement of the artist's arm and brush, a more gestural quality. It is this that owed more to Manessier than Gear and even, perhaps, to the work of Georges Mathieu or Hans Hartung, both known for the way they handled their brush like a swordsman.

With these works Hilton began to gain recognition. Adrian Heath selected him for inclusion in the *Abstract Paintings, Sculptures, Mobiles* exhibition at the AIA gallery in 1951. This was the first survey of post-war British abstract art and, as a result, Hilton was included in a similar exhibition at Gimpel Fils that August. One of his paintings graced the gallery window and all three sold. The Gimpel family had been dealers in Paris for generations and it was in their gallery that Hilton had his first post-war one-person exhibition, in June 1952. The works were the impressionist *tachiste* pieces of the preceding two years and the exhibition was well reviewed. One critic wrote that Hilton's 'colour is admirable and the linear scaffolding of his pictures has an engaging nervous energy'.[20] Hilton and his family had recently moved to North Kensington where he had become friends with Heron, who gave him a rave review in the influential *New Statesman* that was strangely prescient of the work that would come:

Hilton is a natural painter. That is to say he cannot put brush to canvas without creating a splotch, smear, streak, stain or smudge (in other words a 'brushstroke') that is not charged with expressive quality. And when I say expressive, I do not mean expressionist. Hilton is the opposite of that: he is a contemplative among painters. For him the calm virtues of the craft are the main point of the departure: deliberate design; fine, rich and exceptionally varied colour; and a paint texture that shows an equal variety and inventiveness.[21]

Heron's critique clearly reflected conversations with the artist. It seems as if, after years of apprenticeship and even as his work looked too like other peoples' to command real respect, Hilton had arrived at a mature and fully-rounded idea of what he wanted in and from a painting.

Though still obliged to work at a framers, Savages, to make ends meet, Hilton himself felt he had arrived. 'Given a stretch of a few months or a year in which to paint', he wrote to his mother at the beginning of 1953, 'I stand a pretty good chance of coming to the fore. I do not think this is an idle boast … I have the beginnings of a reputation.' He told her of new artist friends – Heron, William Scott and Peter Lanyon – and of prospects for future exhibitions.[22] However, his wife recalled that it was at this time and, apparently, as a reaction to this growing respect that, 'as if to protect his own uncompromising vision, Roger began to react abusively to the world which had begun to make friendly advances to him'.[23]

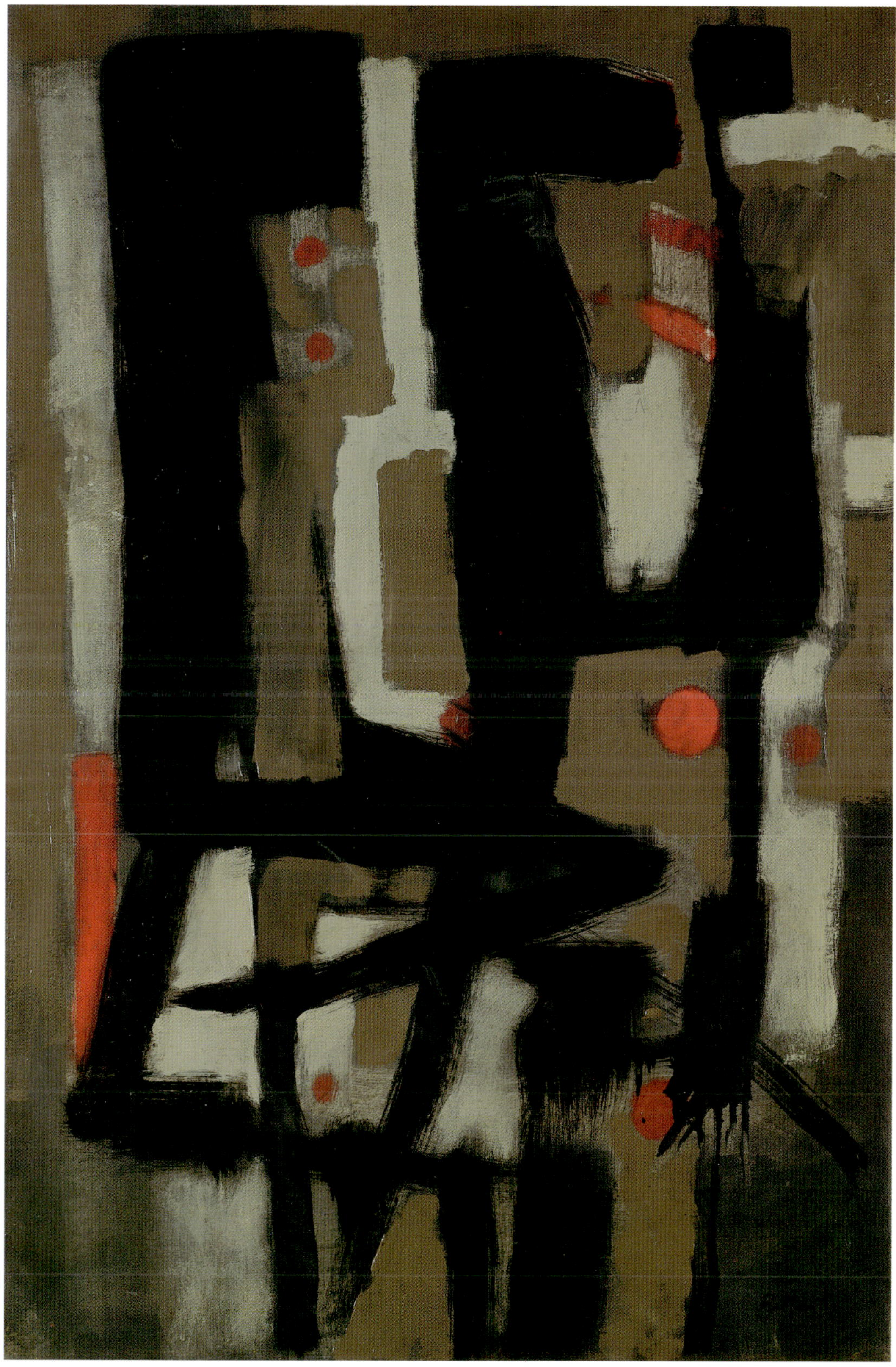

2
1953–1954

Among the artists whom Hilton told his mother he had recently got to know was the Dutchman Constant A. Nieuwenhuys, generally known simply as Constant. Constant was a member of the avant-garde group Cobra, and Hilton no doubt met him through Stephen Gilbert, a Scottish member of the group who had remained Hilton's great friend from Slade School days. Gilbert had lived in Paris since 1945. Cobra was an affiliation of artists from the Netherlands, Belgium, France and Denmark who, in the wake of the Nazi occupation, produced an art that was angry, anarchic, humorous and beautiful. Anticipating Jean Dubuffet's *Art Brut* and picking up threads of Surrealism, their violently gestural paintings of distorted figures and wild creatures, real and imagined, displayed their interest in the art of children, non-Western cultures and the insane. Unlike their contemporaries in the United States, Cobra artists were overtly political. Hilton met Constant at a time when the Dutchman's art was changing radically in terms of its appearance, though an underlying ideology remained consistent. Constant had been the theorist of Cobra, but the group disbanded in 1951, the year in which he visited Hilton at least twice. Between 1952 and 1953 he spent a considerable time in London where he 'chiefly wandered around the city'. Like that of Gilbert, his painting would develop along with his ideas about art, space and society until he was producing modernist architecture, continuing the utopian project of Le Corbusier and the Bauhaus.

The impact of Constant on Hilton's art is clear. In January 1953, he produced a long, horizontal painting of overlaid, soft-edged squares of colour. It was, according to Heron, the last 'in the "impressionist" non-figurative style'. The works that followed that summer were dramatically different. *June 1953* (fig.13) is one of the earliest. The paintings he produced over the next eighteen months to two years consist of a small number of forms, each of a single colour. The forms can be simple or complex, never geometrically precise and always contained within clear boundaries. However elaborate the composition, the shapes of colour never overlap but intersect, generally with a thin boundary of bare canvas between them. The colours can be simple – red, black and white, for example – but can also be a little unexpected. Throughout his career, Hilton's work would be distinguishable by his idiosyncratic palette. There would be no mixing of paint, each colour applied pure. The application was thick, fluent and delicate, with the use of a palette knife. As a result, each area of paint seems like a three-dimensional entity in itself, like a piece of collage. This physical aspect, their underlying theory and intention all served to relate the works, and their maker, to the Constructivist tradition that was enjoying a late flourish in Britain at that time.

For a while, Constant made paintings similar to these works in form if not in colouring, as did Stephen Gilbert. All owed a debt to the paintings of Serge Poliakoff with their interlocking areas of boldly applied paint, an example of which

13
June 1953 1953
Oil on canvas 91.5 × 71

Scottish National Gallery of Modern Art, Edinburgh

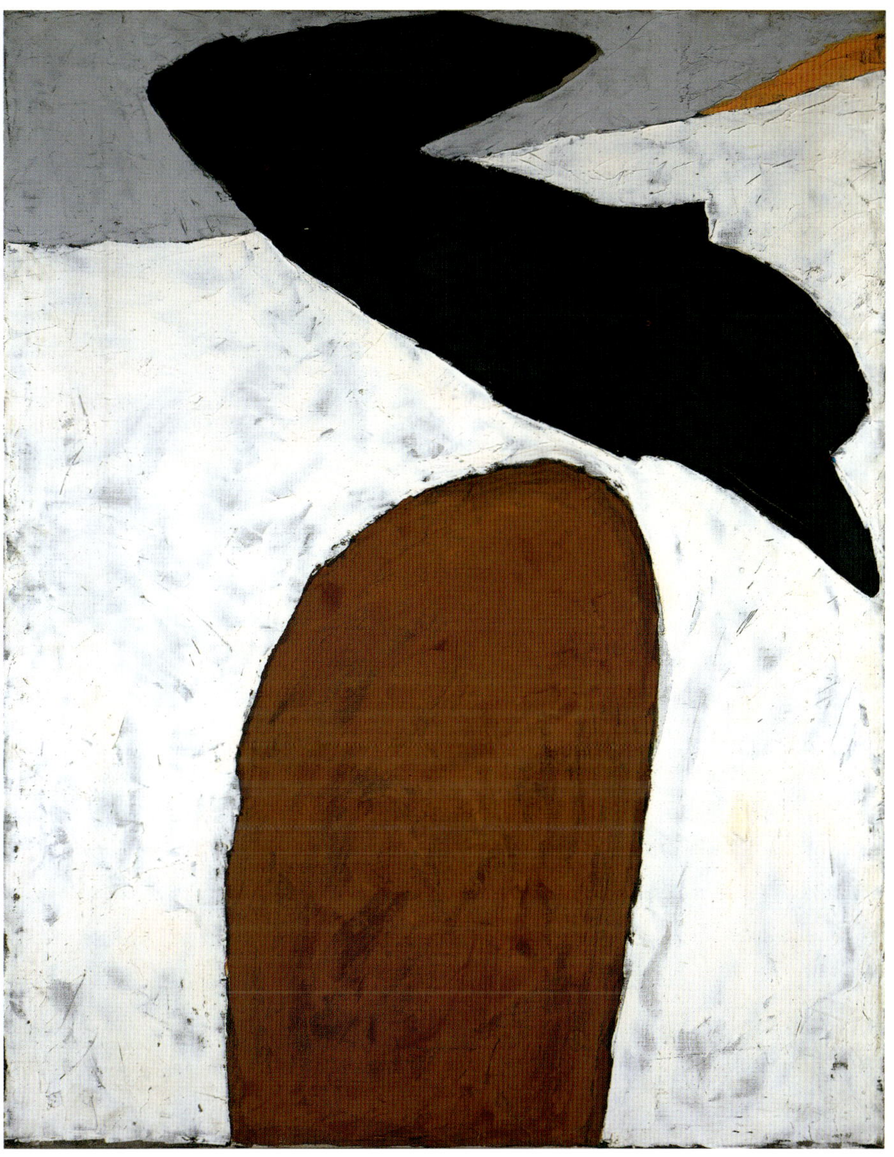

Hilton might have seen in the March 1953 issue of *Art d'aujourd'hui*.[1] Constant was a crucial inspiration for Hilton not only for his own painting and ideas but also for the tradition of abstract painting and theory that he opened up for his British colleague. What had happened in early 1953 to cause such a change in Hilton's work was that, not long after they met, in February 1953 he and Constant had made a trip to Amsterdam. There they saw the works of Piet Mondrian at the Stedelijk Museum. Though known in Britain in the 1930s, there was little opportunity for direct contact with Mondrian's work in the years immediately following the war. In fact, Hilton's discovery coincided with a revival of interest in pre-war adventures in abstraction. In 1953 the painter Adrian Heath published his small book, *Abstract Painting: It's Origins and Meaning*, which traced the development and provided short commentaries on the main protagonists, including Mondrian and the Russian Kasimir Malevich. Though Hilton himself, and subsequent commentators, identified Mondrian and Constant as the inspiration for his change of

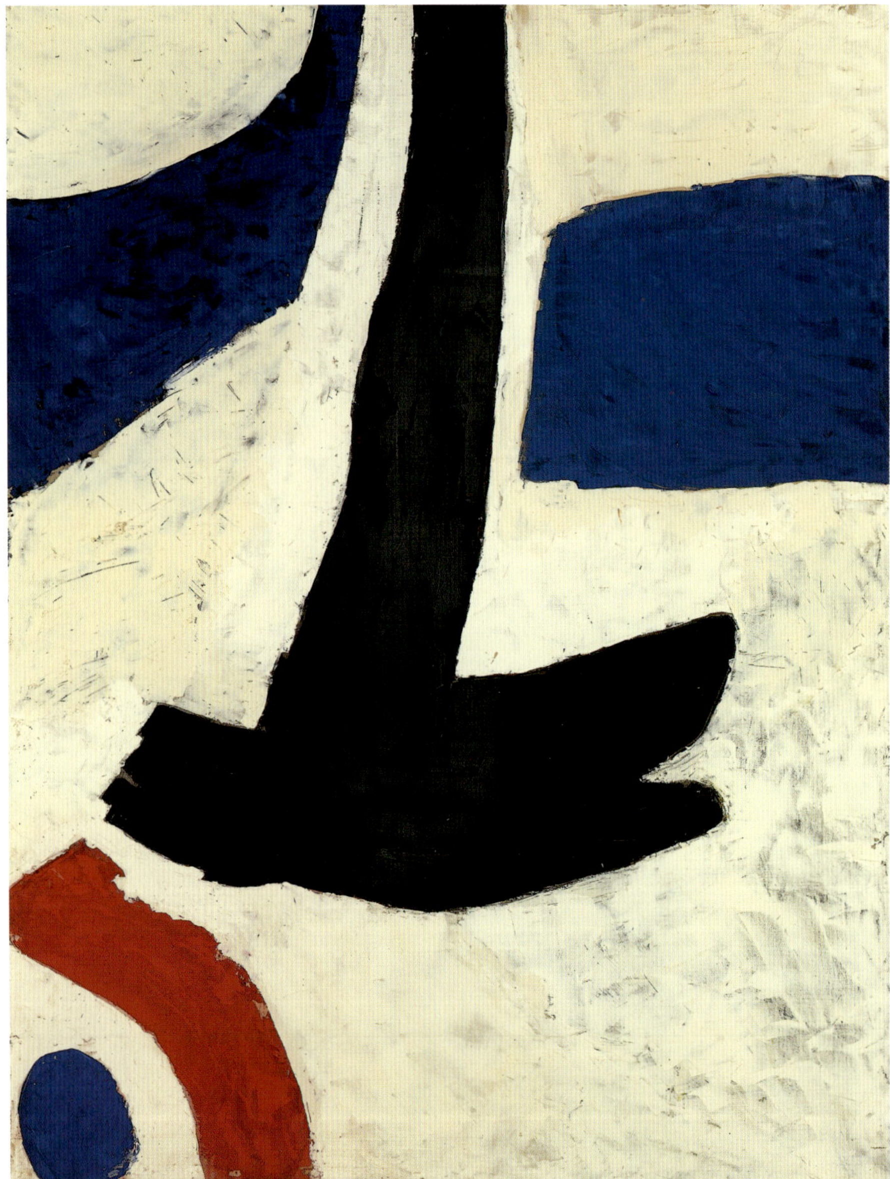

direction, the works themselves would suggest that Malevich was of equal importance. Some of the formal issues were common to both Mondrian and Malevich but the relationship between the different forms in Hilton's compositions and the range of colours relate his paintings most strongly to the Russian's.

What Hilton gained from these past heroes of modernist painting and from their mediator, Constant, was an appreciation of the challenge of creating an art in which forms and colour occupied a single plane without creating the illusion of depth. The complexity of his forms demonstrates the degree to which he wished to push the tolerance of such pictorial flatness. While Mondrian tested himself with parallel and perpendicular lines, risking the creation of narrow recessed areas, Hilton deployed dynamic forms. So the darker form in *June 1953* (fig.13) turns as if it is an enlarged brushstroke and risks appearing as if doubling back on itself into an illusionistic space. Similarly, the central, hammer-like form in *July*

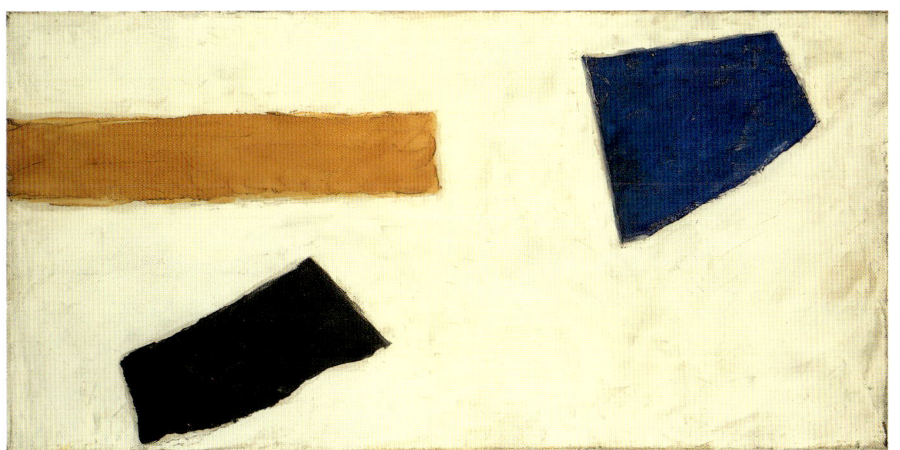

1953 (fig.14) seems to hang as if ready to swing. These works are pregnant with formal tension: not only between the painted figure and the ground of the canvas but also between the different painted forms, each placed in a relationship to the others to create maximum tension as if held by magnetic force. The success of these works, and the context by which they were understood, was reflected in the fact that *July 1953* was acquired by the Stedelijk Museum, Amsterdam, in October that year.

December 1953 (fig.15) is probably the work most like those of Malevich. Three irregular-shaped islands of colour – black, yellow ochre and rich blue – seem to float in a sea of white. In fact, the metaphor of sea and islands is undermined by the narrow glimpses of canvas between the forms, so that all four – the areas of black, yellow, blue and white – are read as independent masses of colour. The work is typical in the emphasis Hilton places on the evident working of the paint, the clarity of the brushwork. (Contrary to common belief, Mondrian also left the mark of the brush evident in his compositions.) *December 1953* is unusual, however, in its deployment of forms completely surrounded by another colour. Generally, Hilton brought the edges of the support into the equation. The role of the edge would, like the relationship between figure and ground, become a *leit-motif* in debates about abstract painting during the 1950s. In contrast to compositions in which the main feature sits at the centre of the canvas, anchoring forms to the edges of the field of action helped defy the tendency of colours and shapes to create illusions of depth. It also served to suggest a world outside the canvas, in that the ragged-edged forms appear to continue beyond the frame.

As Alloway pointed out, by appearing to reach beyond the bounds of the canvas Hilton set out to achieve his goal of making a painting that acted upon actual space rather than one that simply illustrated or created the illusion of space, or in his own words, 'a kind of catalyst for the activisation of the surrounding space'.[2] Hilton wrote:

I have moved from the sort of so-called non-figurative painting where lines and colours are flying about in an illusory space; from pictures which still had depth, or from pictures which had space in them; from spatial pictures in short, to space-creating pictures. The effect is to be felt outside rather than inside the picture: the picture is not to be primarily an image, but a space-creating mechanism.

It was this key aspect of Hilton's approach that led him to become associated with a group of 'Constructionists' who were continuing the project of Constructivism that had been successful in Britain in the 1930s. This group came together in a series of small exhibitions at the home of Adrian Heath and most notably in the 1954 publication *Nine Abstract Artists*, for which Alloway provided the introduction. In fact, Alloway's essay made it clear that he did not see them as a consistent group, and separated out three painters who, he wrote, 'represent … irrational expression by *malerisch* means': William Scott, Terry Frost and Hilton. He clearly felt greater affinity with the others.

In fact, one can discern a common purpose and technical concern among these artists' work. Hilton's desire for a non-representational painting that activates the space it occupies through its apparent projection out into that space was achieved literally by Victor Pasmore, for example, whose contribution included shallow reliefs in which areas of flat colour were made to stand a few millimetres proud of the main support of the work. Hilton acknowledged this affinity whilst also insisting on the maintenance of the parameters of each practice: 'In this penetration of outer space painting is, in a way, encroaching upon sculpture. This is why many painters have turned to actual constructions in space. I think it is not necessary to do the sculptor's job for him.'[3]

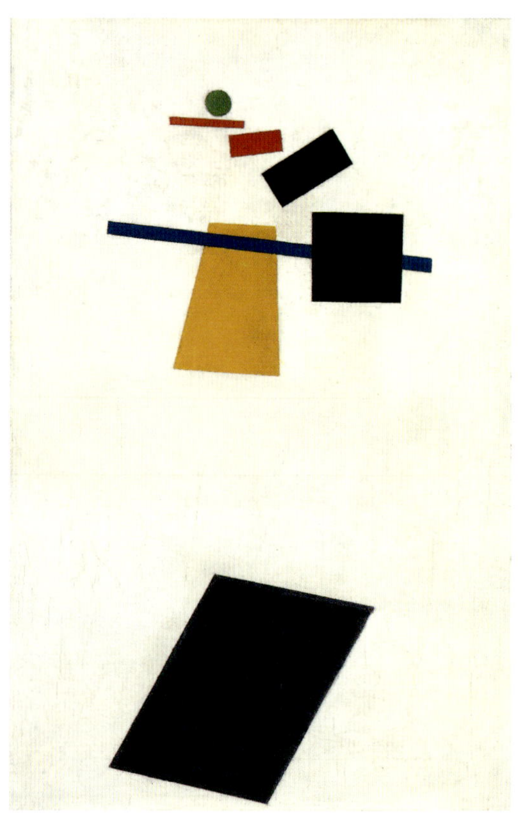

16
Kasimir Malevich
Suprematism: Painterly Realism of a Football Player (colour masses in the fourth dimension) 1915
Oil on canvas
69.8 × 44.1
Stedelijk Museum, Amsterdam

Each of the *Nine Abstract Artists* contributed a statement. In his, Hilton described the artist as an existential hero, 'swinging out into the void', and associated his ideas about abstraction and space with a rather highfaluting notion of the painter as 'a seeker after truth'. In the published text, this truth appears to relate to the artist's technical concerns (and so echoes to a degree Greenberg's theory of modernism as the reduction of any art form to its essential qualities). In the numerous drafts that Hilton produced and the much longer essay which, he would recall, Alloway 'hacked to bits', it is related to more abstruse notions of the 'search for the philosopher's stone'.[4] He made grand claims for such art:

The combination and arrangement of proportions, of colours of different strengths but which at the same time are held to the surface of the canvas so that there is an equivalent force radiating from the whole picture creates a unity which is at once dynamic and static and allows the painter to experiment with forces which seem to bear a relationship to the real problems of human existence, not consciously, but by intuition.[5]

The impression gained from these texts is of a utopian, abstract theory that Hilton struggled to translate into words. It may be that he was trying to articulate, and perhaps adapt, a theory he had himself heard from Constant. The evident confusion of his writings may also reveal the reason why his art would ultimately follow a quite different course to that of Constant and Gilbert.

In a statement from 1952, Constant coined the term 'Spatial Colourism', describing his ambition to develop from his painting the injection of colour into modernist architecture. The architect, he argued, had failed to understand the role of colour in living space and 'spatial colourism' was proposed as a new plastic art, neither painting nor architecture, in which colour and space were seen as indivisible.[6] This was part of a wider return to the pre-war modernist idea of col-

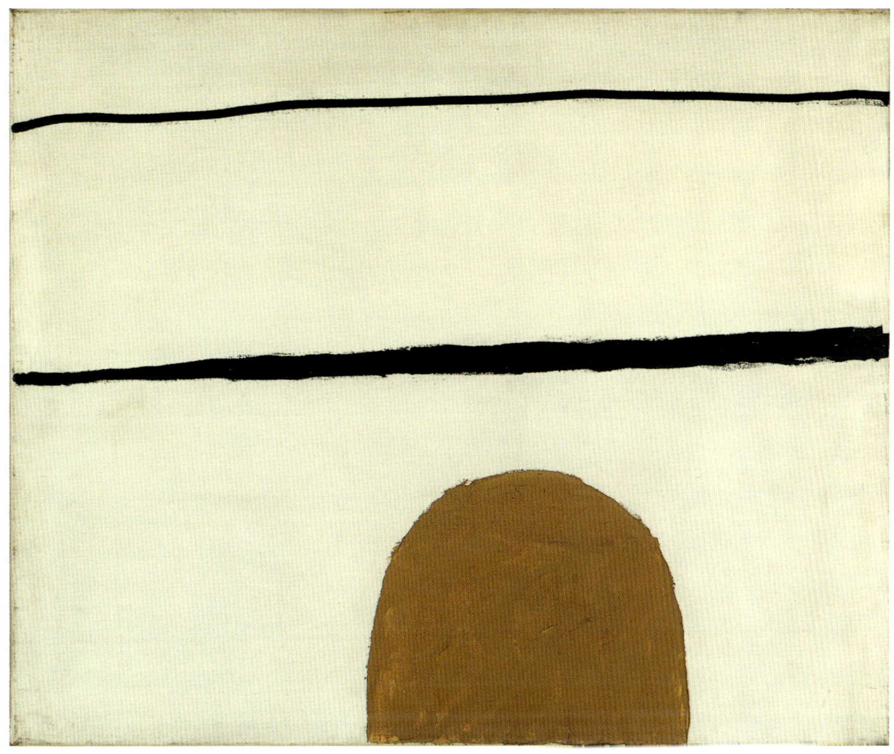

laboration between artist and architect. Gilbert followed a similar path to Constant, from the wild figuration of Cobra, through 'space-creating' abstract painting, to fully-fledged architecture. Hilton was probably a crucial conduit for the de Stijl revival in Britain. His friend David Lewis, who as secretary to Barbara Hepworth in St Ives had direct access to one of the few Mondrian paintings in Britain, wrote a small book on the artist and, inspired by these ideas, retrained in architecture in Leeds where he collaborated with a similar-minded architect, Peter Stead. In St Ives, several artists close to Lewis made sculptures that were, effectively, three-dimensional Mondrians and the whole revival was given extra impetus and affirmation by a major exhibition of the artist's work at the Whitechapel Art Gallery in August 1955.

Hilton showed at the small, short-lived Symon Quinn Gallery that Stead established. Along with a second exhibition at Gimpel Fils in April 1954, which he later described as 'neo-plastic with expressionist overtones', this was the only other display of the austere works of 1953–4.[7] Located in an upstairs space in Huddersfield, Yorkshire, the Symon Quinn Gallery was – rather unexpectedly – one of the few places in Britain outside London to show contemporary abstract art. Hilton was included in the Symon Quinn inaugural exhibition, Romantic Abstraction, and had a solo show there almost a year later in September 1955. The catalogue essay by David Lewis was republished in the Italian periodical *Arti Visive*. This event was as far as Hilton went towards architecture as his paintings were shown not against the wall but suspended between vertical poles so that the canvases were like screens 'filling the room with a sort of picture-grid'. It would, Heron wrote, 'have been admired … by the most theoretical followers of the later Mondrian'.[8] The logical next step might have seemed to have been into architecture itself. Certainly Constant, with whom Hilton maintained an important correspondence during 1953, seems to have assumed that was the ultimate goal

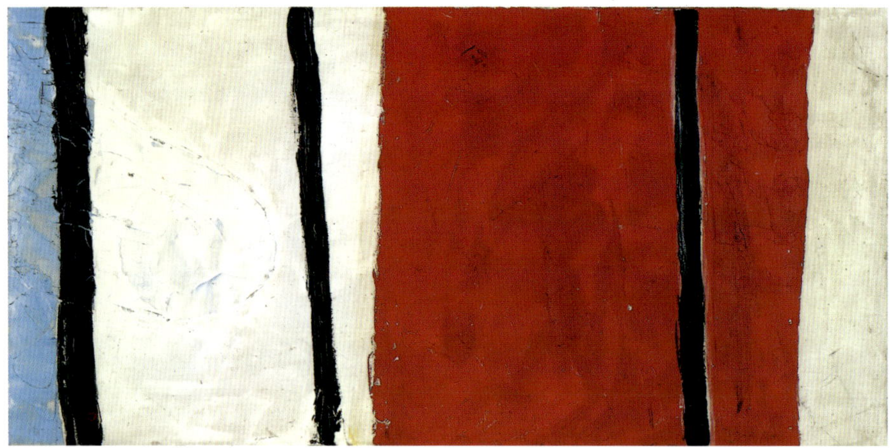

and tried to steer Hilton's painting in that direction. One letter from the autumn of 1953 urged him to avoid the irregular shapes that intruded from the edges of the canvas and to employ instead rectangular forms in order to relate the composition to the shape of the canvas and then to the wall and, ultimately, to make connection with architecture itself. In fact, Hilton was at that time producing a number of long, thin paintings made up of bands of colour. He never, however, abandoned the ragged edges and nervous line that characterised all his forms.

During 1955, stimulated by the interaction of the artists associated with *Nine Abstract Artists* and by the British branch of the abstract *Groupe Espace*, plans were being made for an exhibition in which artists and architects would collaborate. Hilton took part in early discussions of what would become the milestone *This is Tomorrow*, but he withdrew from a collaboration with sculptor Robert Adams and so ended his association with Constructivist circles. Instead, he would develop the aspects of his work that had resisted the pull of Constant and the Constructivists and seems to have so antagonised Alloway: his irregular, asymmetrical forms, his energetic, wobbly line and his unpredictable composition. As Heron pointed out, Hilton had

Failed entirely to conceal the purely expressive, gesticulating side of his creative self. … His intention was … to suppress all the untidy feelings which the habitually lopsided balance of his forms, the 'messy' troweling of pigment and the spluttering charcoal scribbles might lead us to suppose were integral to his artistic personality. Yet in all the works of this period … the forms have the same qualities of raggedness and asymmetry; they are blunted, round-cornered, moth-eaten at the edges … Despite all their training Hilton's forms break ranks and wave a scraggy arm at one wildly; or let their heavy heads hang down, like lifeless scarecrows.[9]

As well as these formal expressions of what Heron liked to see as Hilton's artistic personality, there was another, even less Constructivist pull at play. An unusual but key work from Hilton's so-called Neo-Plastic period of 1953–4 is *August 1953* (fig.19). At first glance it appears to be a derivative of Malevich's compositions of shapes of strong, if not primary, colours floating in a white field. As one looks at it, however, and especially if one recalls the idea of Hilton's paintings framing a section of some larger form, the shapes coalesce into the image of a female torso. Charles Harrison has challenged such a reading on the grounds of the success of Hilton's management of the figure-ground relationship. When viewed directly rather than in reproduction, he argued, the fact that the work is a constructed arrangement of independent blocks of colour is unavoidable. In contrast,

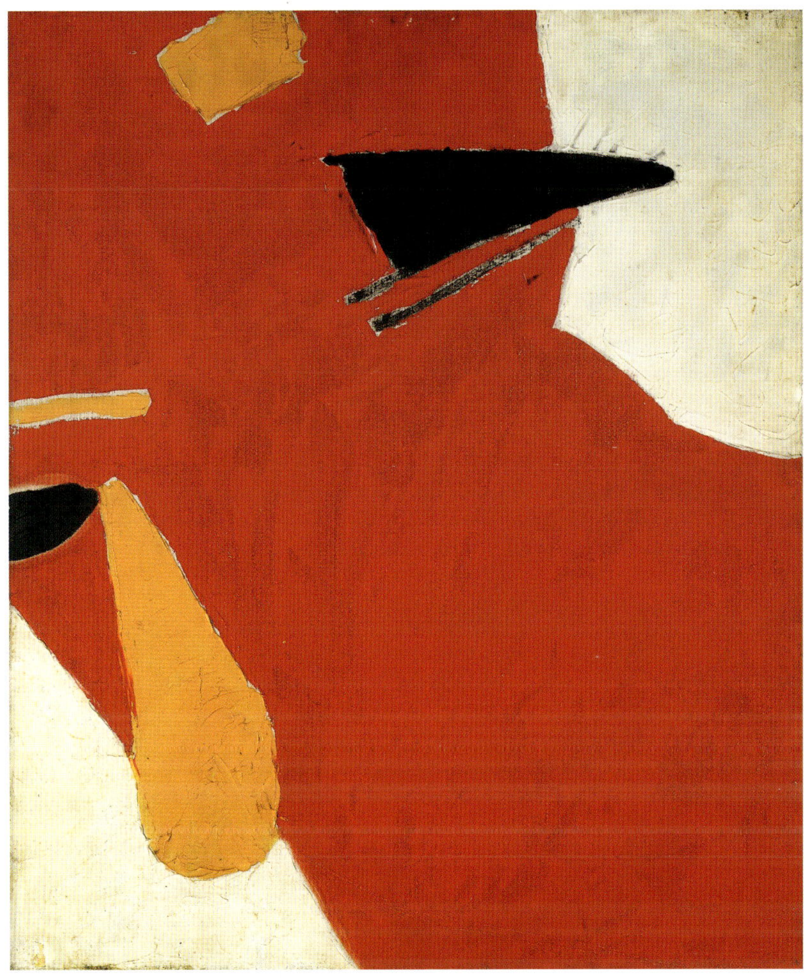

to see the image as a body is to see the forms located in an illusionistic space.[10] In fact, this may be Hilton's intention and challenge to himself. To what degree can one include a human element while abiding by the rules of current formalist practice?

Enlightened by *August 1953*, we might then look differently at other works of this kind. *February 1954* (fig.20) has also been read in terms of the female form – presumably red torso, black legs and breasts – though more alluded to through fragments than represented directly. Perhaps the rhetorical question is: with how little can the human form be suggested? *Painting 1954* (fig.21) would appear to be a demonstration of the way in which Hilton used complex, interlocking shapes to explore the bounds of possibility of juxtaposing colours without creating illusionistic space. Heron held it up as such in his important essay, 'Introducing Roger Hilton', addressed to an American audience in 1957. In light of this buried figuration, however, one might read an erotic subtext into the work, which might now seem to be about sexual (as opposed to simply, formal) penetration. As we shall see, this would become a continual and consistent aspect of Hilton's work, a delicate balance – indeed tension – between luscious paint surfaces, wobbly lines and suggestions of the eroticised body. It was through this subtle negotiation that he repeatedly achieved an art of sensual and sensory pleasure.

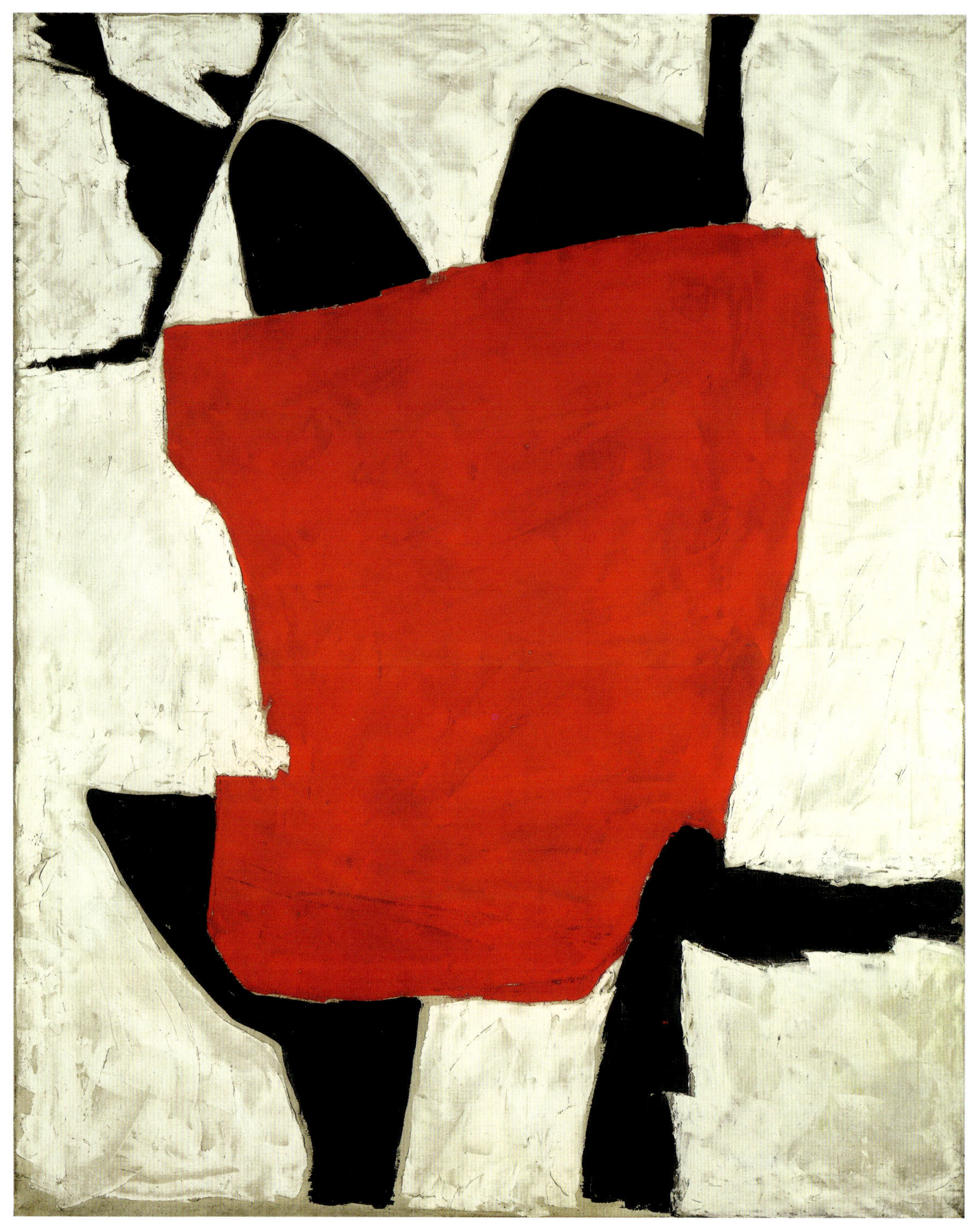

20
February 1954 1954
Oil on canvas
127 × 101.5

Tate

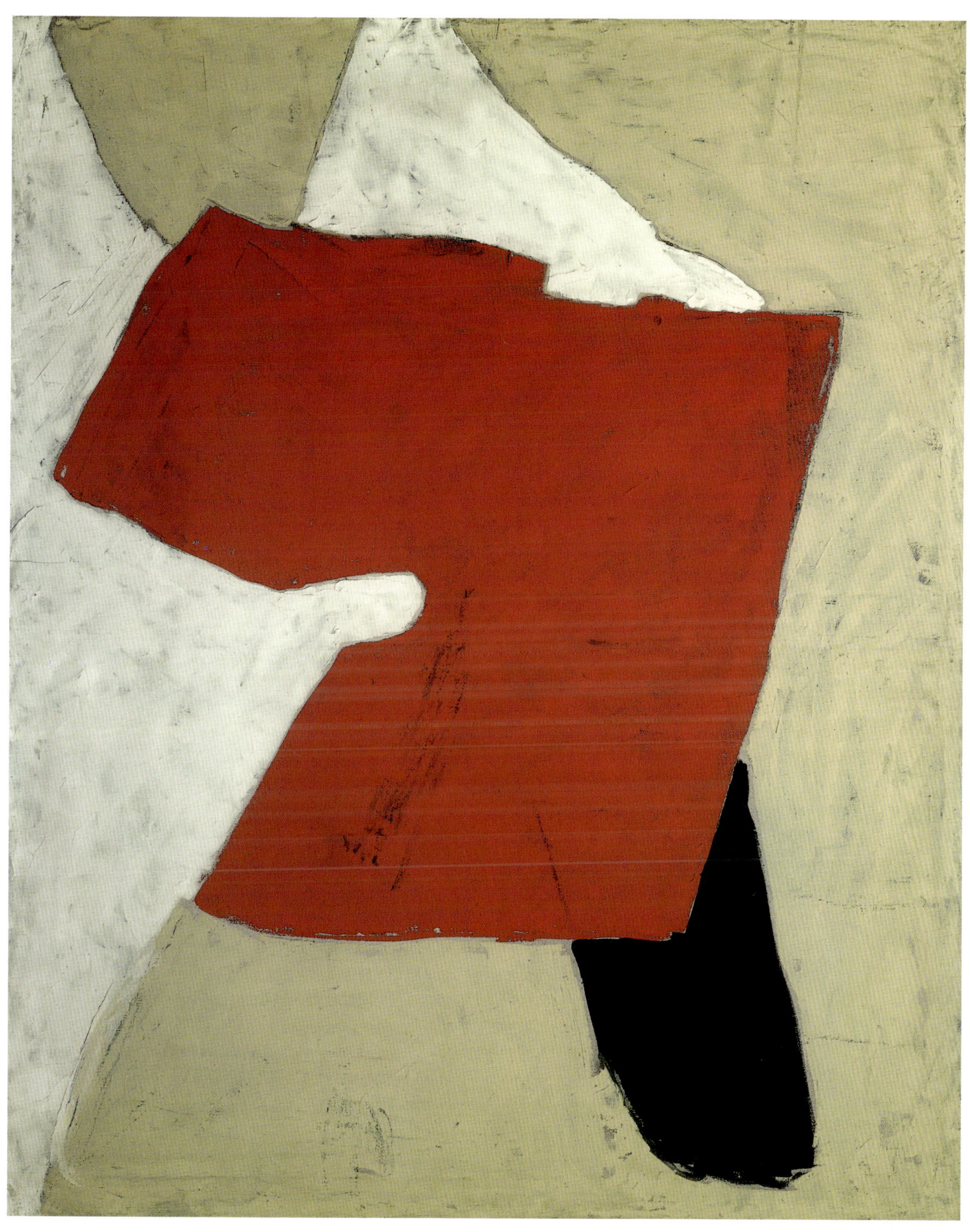

21
Painting 1954 1954
Oil on canvas
127 × 101.6

Arts Council Collection

It is apparent from his paintings that Hilton made a clear decision to distance himself from the austere abstraction that had led him in the direction of Bauhausian architecture. The experience had confirmed the importance for him of paint and painting. As Heron had pointed out, Hilton's art had never become the 'ascetic', 'dried-out' and 'flat' work that Alloway accused it of being. The apparently irrational, impulsive approach and evident love of the medium of paint was always obvious and it was this that Hilton now played up all the more. The experience of making the works of 1953–4 (which still remain among his strongest) had clarified what he did not want to give up. That did not mean, however, that Hilton knew exactly which direction in which to move in terms of representation. As a consequence, his art of the following few years appears much more changeable in terms of content and treatment and a lot less consistent in terms of quality. It is a characteristic of Hilton's career overall that there are certain periods when he seems barely able to put a foot wrong and others when the odd great work stands out among a larger array of less successful compositions.

Hilton's dilemma was explored and shared through a correspondence with the painter Terry Frost. The two had met in the early 1950s. Frost was based in St Ives. Hilton had become socially associated with the artists in the Cornish town, which was then a powerful centre for contemporary art production equal, probably, to London. His friend and advocate, Patrick Heron, spent his summers in St Ives, and had introduced him to other artists such as Peter Lanyon, Bryan Wynter and William Scott. Hilton, however, resisted the attractions of St Ives. His wife recalled: '"What is this Cornwall?" Roger would say, testily, as if he feared he was going to be sucked into a provincialisation he dreaded.'[1] In 1955, however, Hilton and his family visited Cornwall and the following year he stayed with Heron in his new home in West Penwith, beyond St Ives. He even rented one of the Piazza Studios in the town. Hilton met the poet W.S. Graham, recently returned to Penwith, who became an important friend, and his visits to Cornwall became more frequent.[2] He bought a small cottage near Nancledra, in the heart of the Penwith moors, and he rented a small studio near the harbour in Newlyn, where he painted during the summers of 1957, 1958, 1959 and possibly 1960.[3]

Ironically, from 1954 Frost was spending most of his time in Leeds, where he was the Gregory Fellow in painting at the university. This offered the opportunity for he and Hilton to exchange ideas and concerns by correspondence. The concentration of the letters in 1955 and their content suggests that, as well as friendship and distance, Hilton needed to articulate his artistic quandary. In spring 1955, he advised Frost that he was 'getting into something new … I am tired of non-figuration. Though they may not be overtly figurative I am going in future to introduce if possible a more markedly human element in my pictures while endeavouring at the same time to dispose their forms in a space creating man-

22
November 1955 1955
Oil on canvas
111.8 × 86.4

Swindon Museum and Art Gallery

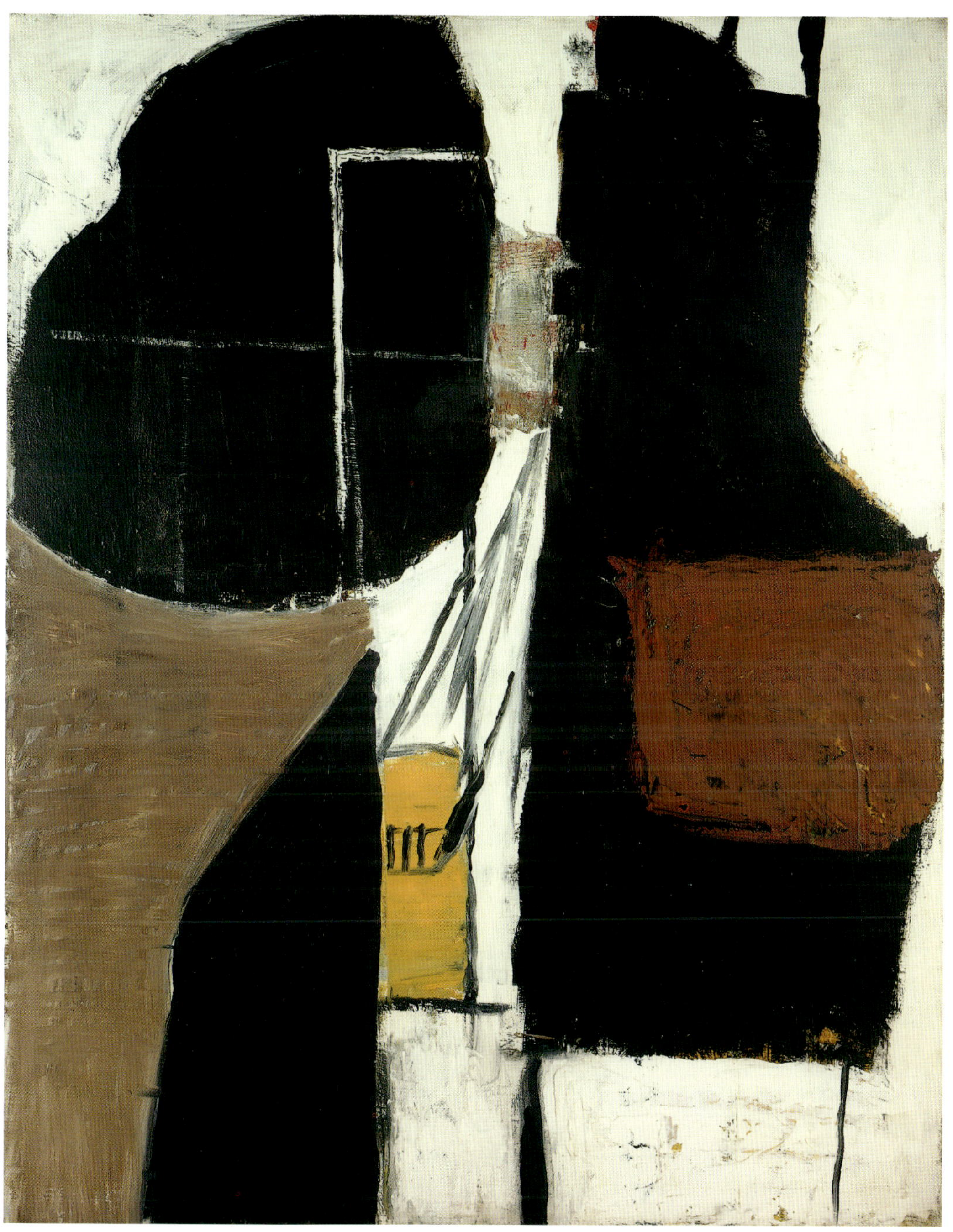

ner'.[4] He did indeed, in mid-1955, produce a series of works in which blocks of colour, mostly roughly square, combined to form human figures. The manner of the depiction makes clear a debt to the sculptor Kenneth Armitage, a friend of Hilton. The artist was not sure about them, speculating that 'they are probably a flash in the pan. It is too early to say quite what they are but they are certainly figurative in intention, expressionistic, totemic and in fact by all my previous standards thoroughly bad'.[5]

As it turned out these paintings *were* a flash in the pan and, even in retrospect, pretty poor by the standard of Hilton's earlier and subsequent work. It was not much later that he wrote, 'I cannot really defend myself … The attempt to bring back figuration was probably premature. In my case, I am only feeling my way. I think the attempt has already failed. It was a mistake to let Gimp[els] have them.'[6] The degree to which Hilton was unsure how to progress may be reflected in the fact that at the same time as these failed figurative works he was also making 'very sober things, austere practically to the point of extinction'.[7] Reflecting on his uncertainty, however, he effectively described the course his career would take over the coming years:

It is disconcerting not knowing whether my next show will be of chaste abstracts or violent figuration but in any case it will be one or the other. If abstract they will be fulgurent, demonic, tragic, expressionistic, violent, wanton and destructive. It seems to me this is the nature of the time we live in with untold possibilities of destruction, untold possibilities of building a new world.[8]

It is noteworthy that his repositioning was not necessarily an abandonment of the values that had underpinned the Neo-Plastic works of 1953–4. His association of an intended new abstract style with the character of the period – one overshadowed by the potential of the post-war period but also by the bomb and the possibility of total destruction – shows a more nuanced ideological position, perhaps, than the utopianism of Constant.

One of Hilton's anxieties about the work of 1953–4 and the Constructivist, Neo-Plastic project was that it was too much about other painting, 'too much starting from the canvas'.[9] Despite its ideological intentions, he felt his paintings stemmed from others' work, not from his own imagination or, perhaps, from the human figure. Thus he found himself caught in this pull between abstraction and figuration. The progress of his career over the following five to ten years was towards an art in which both could sit comfortably together. In fact, even in 1955 as he contemplated the disappointment of his figurative paintings and the austere pieces, he was capable of producing the occasional highly successful work in which abstract values were maintained while the figure was alluded to.

Though there is nothing specific with which to make the association, it seems natural to read *November 1955* (fig.22), on one level, as representing a pair of figures. It is, equally, a kind of Cubist painting. There is something about the balance of the composition and the relationship of the different areas of colour, particularly the small central rectangle of yellow, that suggests the shallow, interweaving planes of a Cubist composition by Gris, perhaps, or Leger. Almost a year later, in *October 1956* (fig.23), the references to the figure are less ambiguous. Indeed, this looks like a refined version of the aborted series of summer 1955 with a large area of brown superimposed as if to undermine the overly literal nature of the body. So we see an oblong head squeezed hard against the top edge of the canvas and two legs, the tapering one on the viewer's right recalling the women in black stockings painted by William Scott around that time. Towards the left, a row of small curved forms allude to the fingers of a hand and derive, it would appear, from the more recent work of Picasso. It does not seem difficult to see in this painting the sort of figure that might be suggested by Hilton's brief summary of the times in which he lived. He had reintroduced the figure as a rejection of the ascetic 'art about art' of preceding years, but this is a figure that appears threatened and violated, as the large brown form intrudes upon it, and it is scratched, erased and fragmented.

A similar historical metaphor has been suggested for the slightly earlier *December 1955* (fig.24). This work was considered of sufficient importance to be

23
October 1956 1956
Oil on canvas
140 × 127

British Council

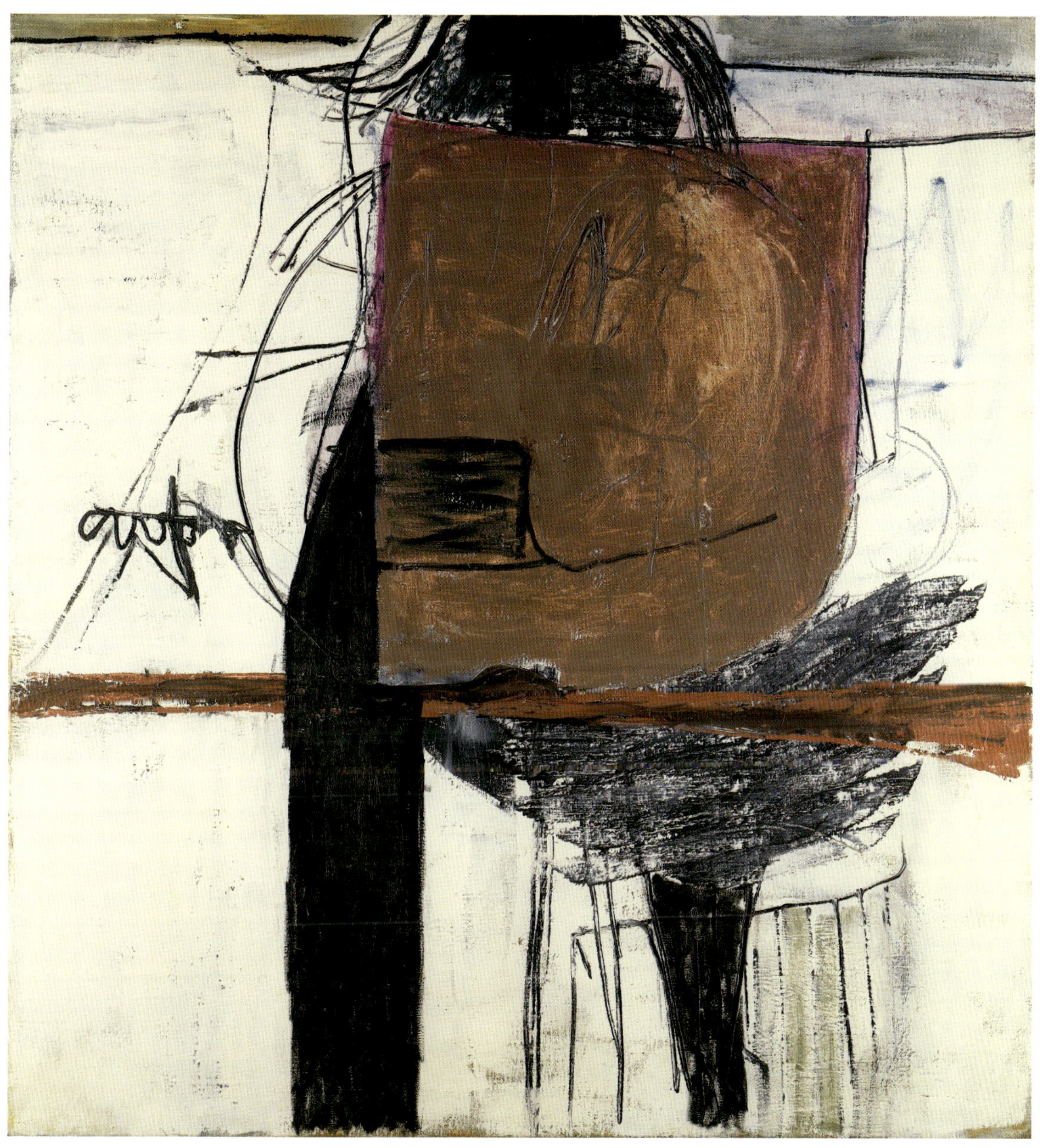

reproduced in Heron's landmark article that introduced Hilton to an American audience. It is still possible to believe that the 'image' of the eponymous centaur was arrived at unconsciously, or accidentally, and perhaps that the subtitle was only suggested when the final painting was observed. Nevertheless, the appending of the label obliges the work to be read in a representational as well as formal way. The work also illustrates how slippery such imagery can be. It is what appears to be the upper part of a body rising up in the top left quarter of the composition that provides its centaur-ness. Were it not for that, the two black forms towards the right would most obviously be seen as allusions to breasts or buttocks even by those unaware of Hilton's propensity for such references. As it is, these forms now become the lower, horse part of the mythical beast. One might go on to relate this work to a broader revival of interest in myth among artists in Britain and the United States. Myths served to provide universal archetypes, free of historically specific political associations, through which artists might address the themes of contemporary culture to which Hilton had referred. In light of that one could, if one wished, see this painting as an image of the human as bestial, apparently raising his arms in triumph, though the colouring creates an impression of *contre jour* that casts such a gesture in a more pathetic, perhaps ironic, light.

In parallel with these semi-figurative works, Hilton continued to produce paintings based on the arrangement of interlocking blocks of colour. Now, however, they were not primary colours but slightly more muted, more earthy hues: black, different whites and a variety of ochres. Though Hilton had always revelled in a luscious paint surface, works such as *April 1956* (fig.25) showed him indulging in a greater degree of painterliness. The basic arrangement is still of solid forms but now the occasional dynamic flourish — a couple of thin black lines near the top edge, a brush heavy with ochre drawn in a semi-circle over a patch of black — breaks up the order. There is also a greater degree of over-painting which has been consciously left evident. As well as giving the colours depth this also reveals the process of painting as gradual and contingent, in contrast to the apparent certainty of the composition and painting in the works of 1953–4. In terms of process, 1956 saw the advent of a practice that would become one of the most important and distinctive aspects of Hilton's painting — the drawing of charcoal over and into the paint — which first appeared in such works as *October 1956* (fig.26). Again, allusions to the human figure seem to emerge, but the artist's

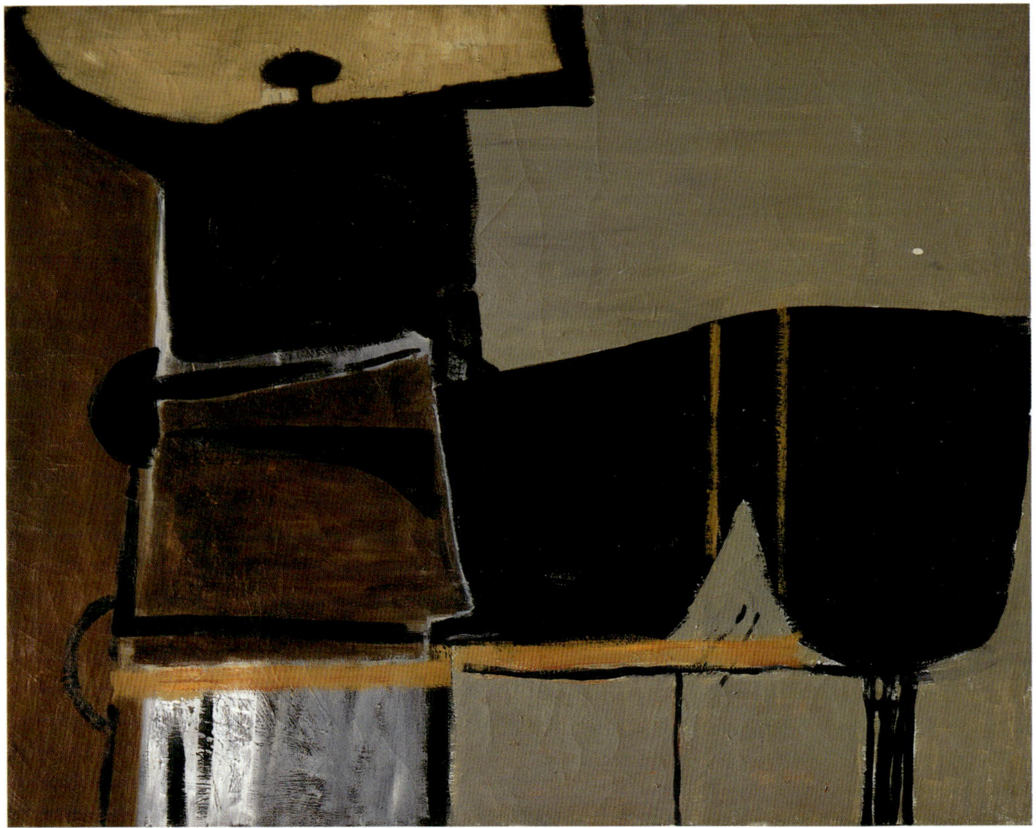

24
*December 1955
(Centaur)* 1955
Oil on canvas
111.8 × 86.4

Private Collection

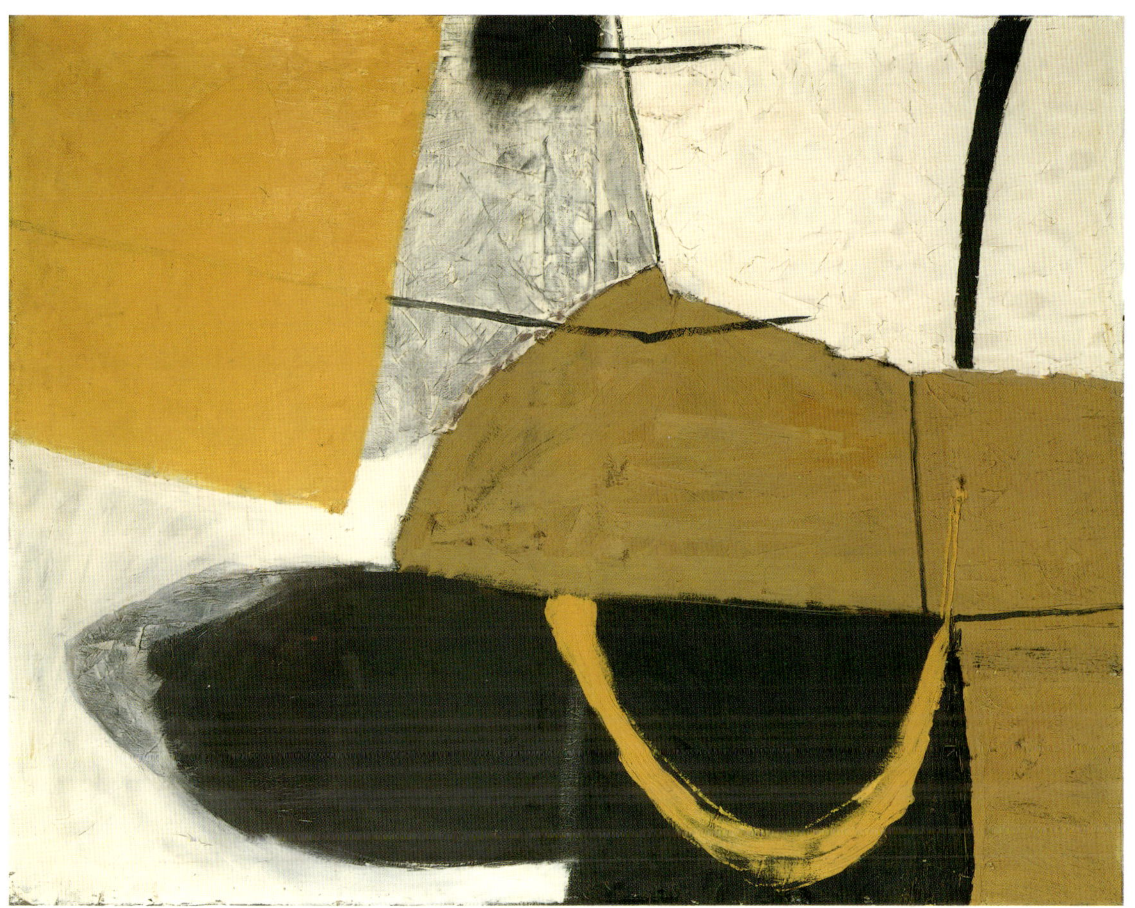

25
April 1956 1956
Oil on canvas
101.5 × 127

Fitzwilliam Museum,
University of Cambridge

range of means when handling the medium provides as powerful an expressive charge as any sort of imagery. The disruption of orthodox hierarchies of materials also serves to give the work a provisional air, as if still in process.

When some of these works were exhibited in Hilton's third and final exhibition at Gimpel Fils in September 1956 several critics discussed them in terms of abstract expressionism. That term had been used very loosely in British critical discourse and was often used literally to describe a form of abstraction that was also expressionistic. In the wake of the exhibition *Modern Art in the United States* at the Tate Gallery that January, however, it had inevitable associations with the group of American artists, most of whose work had then been seen in Britain for the first time. Hilton was aware of their work before then. Scott had visited the main protagonists in New York in 1953 and, through Heron, Hilton had met their leading apologist, Clement Greenberg, who first visited London in 1954. In mid-1955 Hilton wrote to Frost that 'the Americans have made a challenge that cannot be ignored'.[10] Nevertheless, any impact is far from clear. Certainly, the size or scale of work by such artists as Jackson Pollock is not reflected in Hilton's painting, which almost never exceeded six feet and was often smaller. It may be that like Scott, to whose work Hilton's was frequently compared, the sight of the American art merely served to confirm his Europeanness. Hilton had, for some time, been carrying out research in parallel to the Americans. Both Hilton and the Americans were seeking a way forward for painting in the wake of the war and in the wake of Surrealism, Constructivism and of Matisse and Picasso. Each was

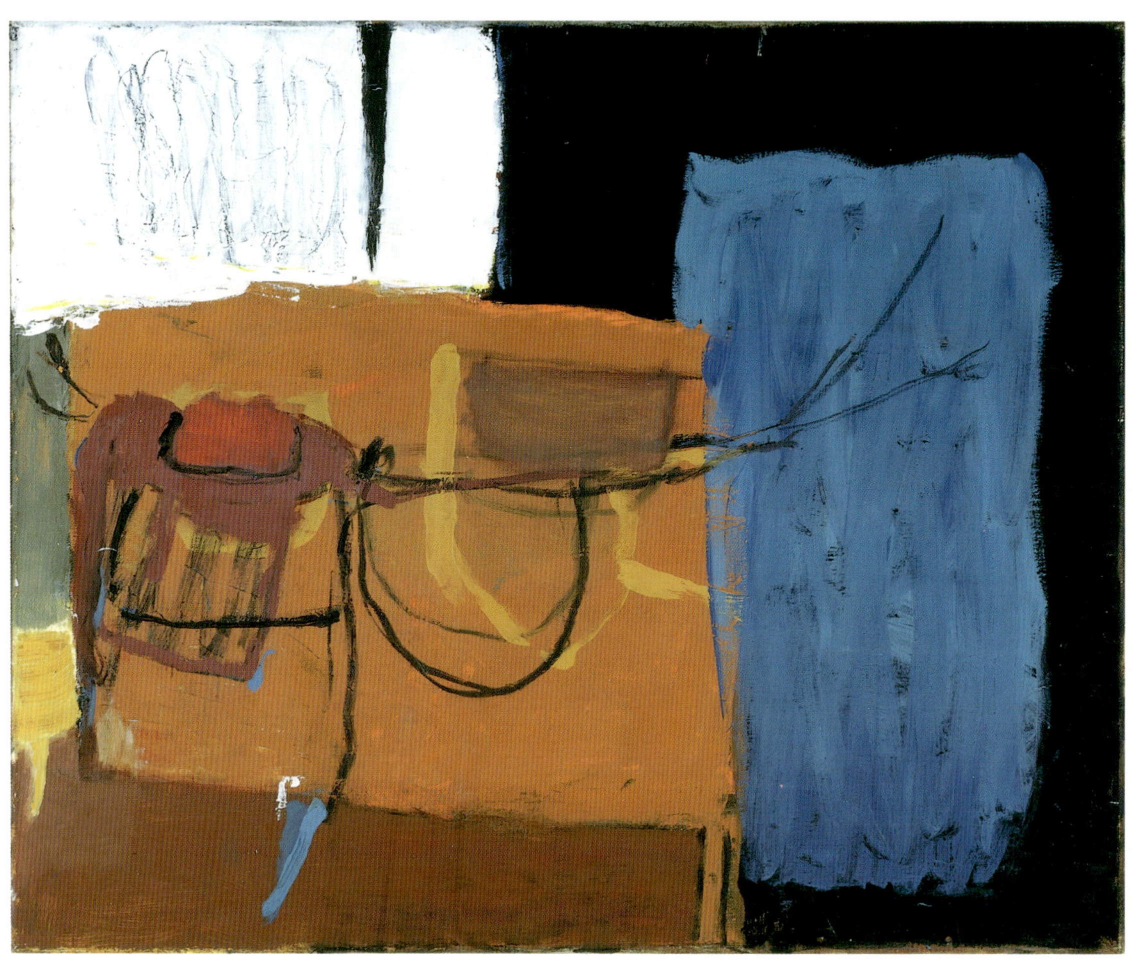

trying to develop an art for their time that expressed humankind's potential for benefit and for brutality, that had a human dimension while resisting the conservatism of illustration and spatial illusion. These were common concerns that American and British artists had shared for some time, just as their advocates – Greenberg and Heron respectively – had arrived at similar but distinct formalist theories of modern painting. They had, in Hilton's own estimation, 'arrived at similar conclusions … by different routes'.[11] In time, he would come to develop an art more radical, and less tasteful, than the Americans'.

Heron proposed that it was St Ives that had an impact on Hilton's work. During 1956, he spent some time working in 2 Piazza Studios, overlooking the beach there. He wrote to Scott: 'Here I am in the provinces in a bigger studio than I've ever had in my life and not an idea in my head. My studio window, which is huge, presents me all day long with a vast panorama of rolling sea. It is difficult to do anything which will shout it down'.[12] He was in St Ives working for the first few months of 1957 as well.[13] Hilton was able to spend so much time in Cornwall because his marriage was gradually disintegrating: 'It is strange to be a batchelor [sic] again after all these years,' he wrote to Scott. 'I would not say it is entirely pleasant'.[14] Whatever the reason for his stay in St Ives, according to Heron it resulted in a change in his work. 'Colour is silkier in tone, subtler in hue. There is an altogether new fluency in the drawing and a greater elegance in the concep-

26
October 1956 1956
Oil on canvas
140 × 127
Southampton City Art
Gallery

27
Blue Newlyn 1958
Oil on canvas
62.5 × 75
Ronnie Duncan Collection

tion; and in the handling', he wrote.[15] These qualities came all the more to the fore when Hilton rented a space by Newlyn harbour.

For the first time, Hilton began to attach labels that invited an association to be made between the painting and some external referent. There are a number of works that have 'Newlyn' in their title. *Blue Newlyn* (fig.27) illustrates with particular verve the new economy that Hilton began to achieve in his work towards the end of the 1950s. It is as if he has managed to combine the simplicity (as opposed to purity) of the Neo-Plastic works with a more impulsive, gestural quality. The result is an economy of means and of image, as the painting consists of only three colours, each applied quickly. Such is the energy with which the paint appears to be applied that it has splashed across the bare canvas towards the sides. The two blocks of different blues seem to have been painted rapidly, and then a few black lines (possibly straight from the tube) added in the most cursory way as a gesture towards containing the forms. These, along with the sweep of deeper blue that passes across the lighter shade, also serve to flatten out the composition to arrest any tendency for the different areas to drop back to create the illusion of space. The old rules still apply. However, the title and the colouring inevitably invite the viewer to read the work as in some way a representation of a place. Specifically, we might find here the blue sea, the difference between harbour water and the open ocean, signalled by the change in tone.

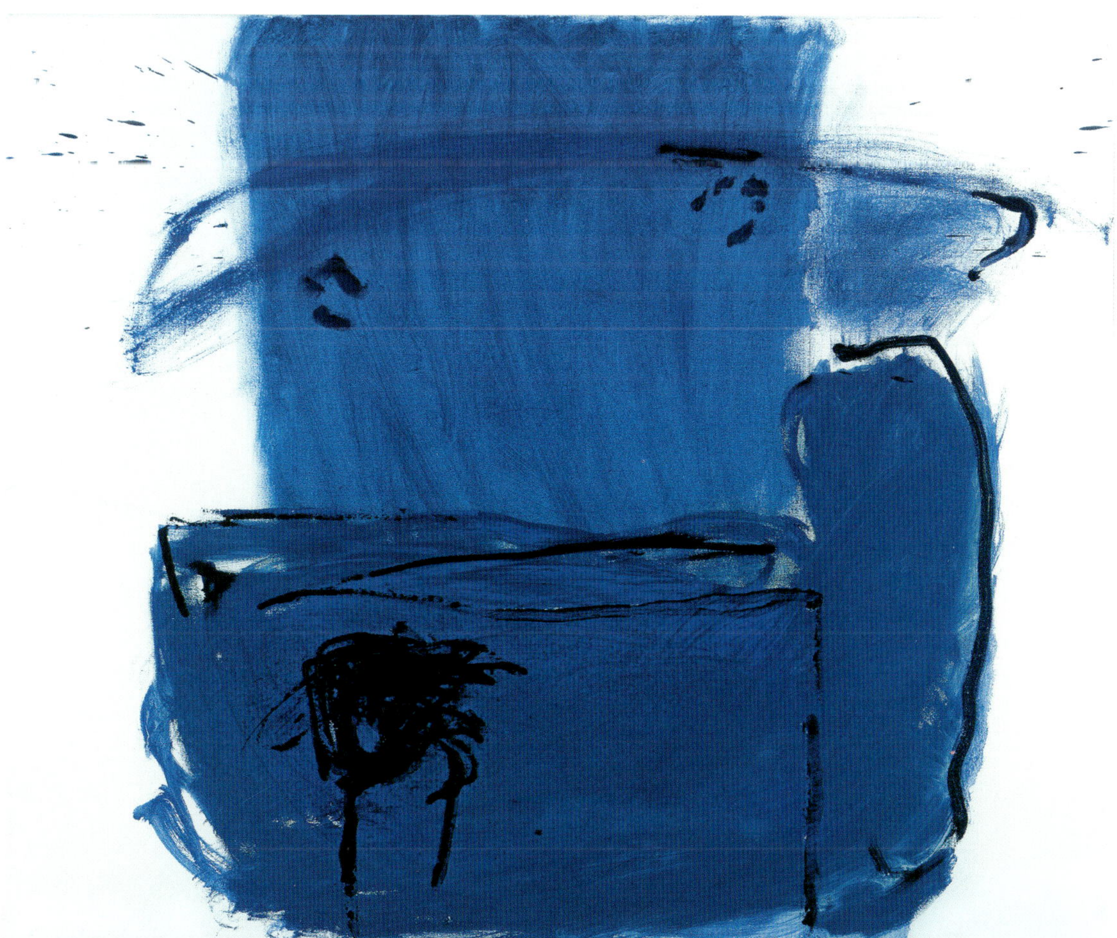

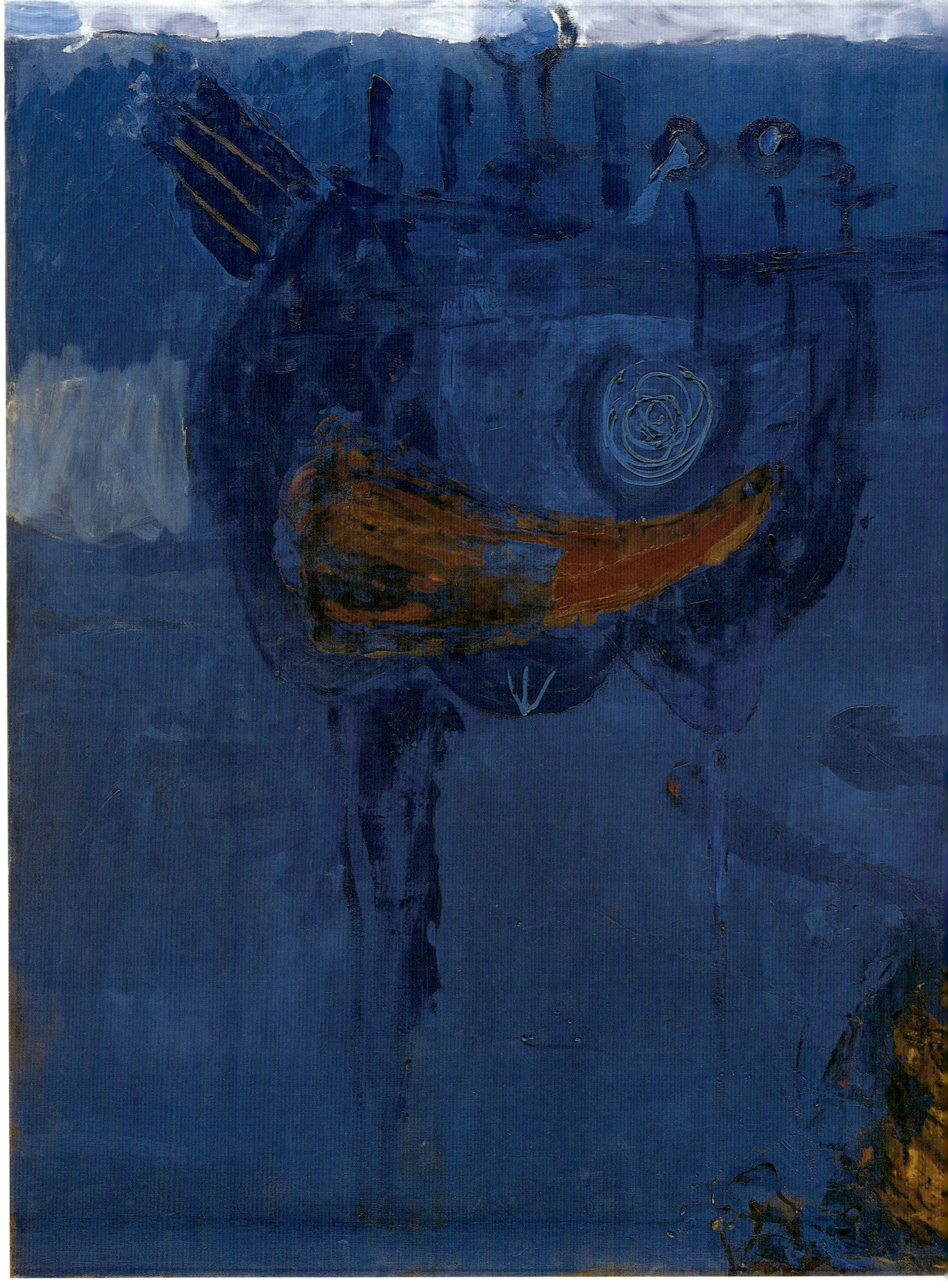

28
The Aral Sea 1958
Oil on canvas
213.4 × 243.8
Private Collection

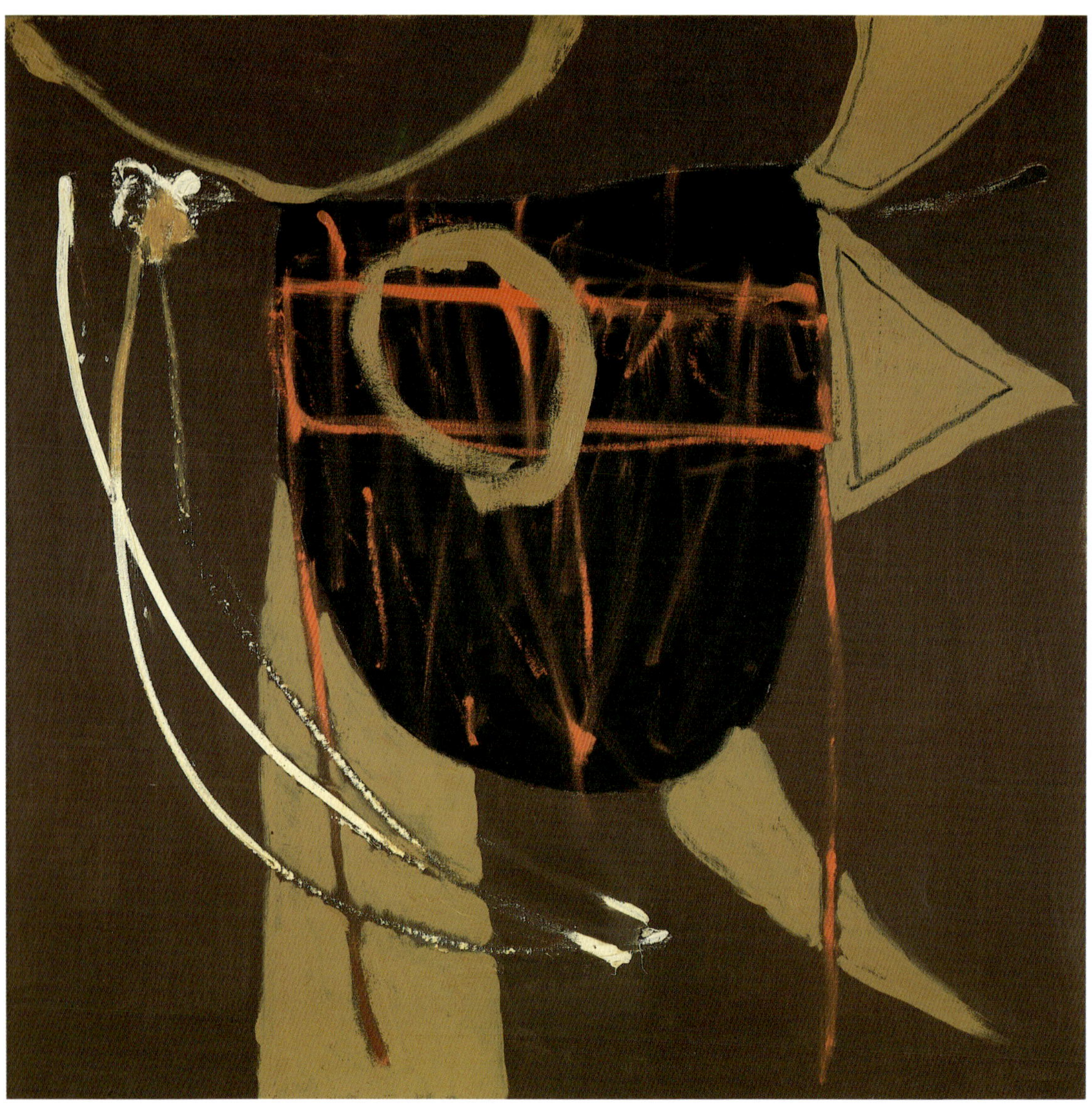

It is the case that Hilton's proximity to the sea coincided with the introduction of new, and appropriate, forms. Boats became something of a favourite though this also relates to Hilton's introduction by Graham to Arthur Rimbaud's poem 'Le Bateau ivre' (the drunken boat). From 1958 Hilton began to attach evocative, if not poetic, titles to his works. One of the first was *The Aral Sea* 1958 (fig.28), a large, deep-blue composition that incorporated an abstracted, spindly legged, evidently female figure. That the work evokes ideas of the ocean, as well as of the erotic, is clear. It seems unlikely that there was any sort of direct relationship with the actual Aral Sea – a large inland sea then in the southern Soviet Union – and perhaps the name was chosen purely for its mysterious, exotic qualities. This seems to be true of a number of Hilton's titles from this period, though most can be related in some way to his seaside environment: *Flying Tamarisk* (fig.29) refers to a shrub common in Cornwall; *Grey Day by the Sea* (a title given to two works) says something, perhaps, about the climate of the Cornish Riviera. Hilton sought to minimise the significance of the titles and explained that he did not

29
Flying Tamarisk, March 1959 1959
Oil on canvas 66 × 66

Psiche & Philip Hughes Trust

intend them to be too specific. Of *Grey Day by the Sea, February 1960* he wrote:

In titling my pictures I took a look at them and wrote down the first thing that came into my head. If nothing came I didn't give it a title. The picture has no more or less to do with the sea or grey days than any other picture in my exhibition though naturally I hope a little of sea and land and grey days and bright days come into all of them.[16]

Nevertheless, *A Strange Route*, *Desolate Beach* and *The Long Walk* are more suggestive titles while *Once Upon a Time* (fig.30) and *Over the Hills and Far Away* actually use narrative clichés to play, perhaps, on the notion of titles suggesting stories. That the image of *Once Upon a Time* seems to suggest female genitalia, if not an anus, makes such titling all the more provocative. Though they did not last, oblique references to the body and its functions would become all the more evident in the next phase of Hilton's development.

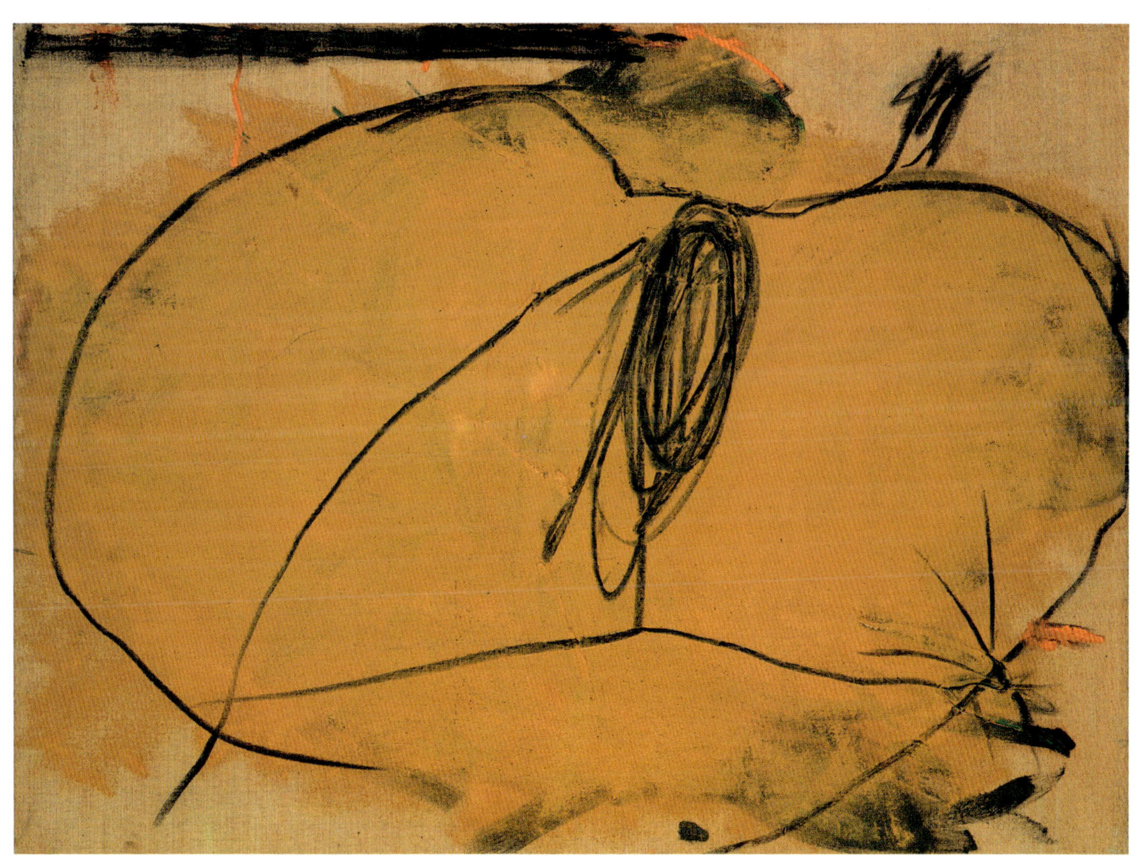

4
1960–1972

The beginning of the 1960s marked a turning point for Hilton. In the late 1950s, he and his wife Ruth gradually grew apart, Hilton spending more and more time in Cornwall. When he was in London, he tended to stay at his studio while she remained at 10 St Ann's Road, North Kensington, the family home since December 1951. Studios had been a problem for Hilton. Ruth later recalled that he had, initially, worked at home, moving from room to room. He rented a space in nearby Ansley Place for about a year, followed by another near Lord's cricket ground in St John's Wood. In 1958 Hilton met the young painter Rosemary Phipps, with whom a committed and, as it would turn out, life-long relationship began.

By this time, he was beginning to get established. Hilton enjoyed the support of the British Council, then the key state supporter of contemporary art. In 1958, the Tate Gallery finally acquired a work. Having initially resisted, in 1959 Hilton joined Waddington Galleries. Victor Waddington was the first dealer in London to offer artists a regular stipend. The modest sum of £360 a year was enough to allow Hilton to give up his part-time teaching at the Central School of Art. He had taught there since January 1954 and had never liked it. It is possible he was not especially good at it, either. Terry Frost later told the story of a summer school at which Hilton stood before a class of art teachers and told them, simply, 'None of you will be an artist as long as you've got a hole in your arse'.[1]

Hilton's autobiographical note, probably drafted in 1960, describes a moment of great confidence and some doubt:

1960
English art took its place as equal to that of France and America, effectively superior to that produced by the French and Italians.
The battle is won for my fellow-combatants, except for a few small pockets of resistance still. The Tate Gallery fell. At the same time, the arrival of Waddington's complicates things. He sells and one earns money, but the danger is one is not thoroughly free …
Successes.
My marriage on the rocks. My wife has found her true love. And as for me?[2]

Despite this uncertainty, from 1960 Hilton worked with extraordinary confidence. It was a productive year, with about sixty paintings completed. More importantly, over the next three years he produced the most distinctive and accomplished work of his career.

In 1958, Hilton provided a statement to accompany his exhibition at the Institute of Contemporary Arts, London. He reused much of it for a similar statement in the catalogue of his one-person exhibition at the Galerie Charles Lienhard in Zurich in 1961. To some extent, these two texts were reaffirmations of his decision in 1955 to abandon the Neo-Plastic style. There is one subtle but crucial difference between the two, however. In 1958, Hilton dismissed the argument

31
March 1960 1960
Oil and charcoal on canvas
101.6 × 152.4

Tate

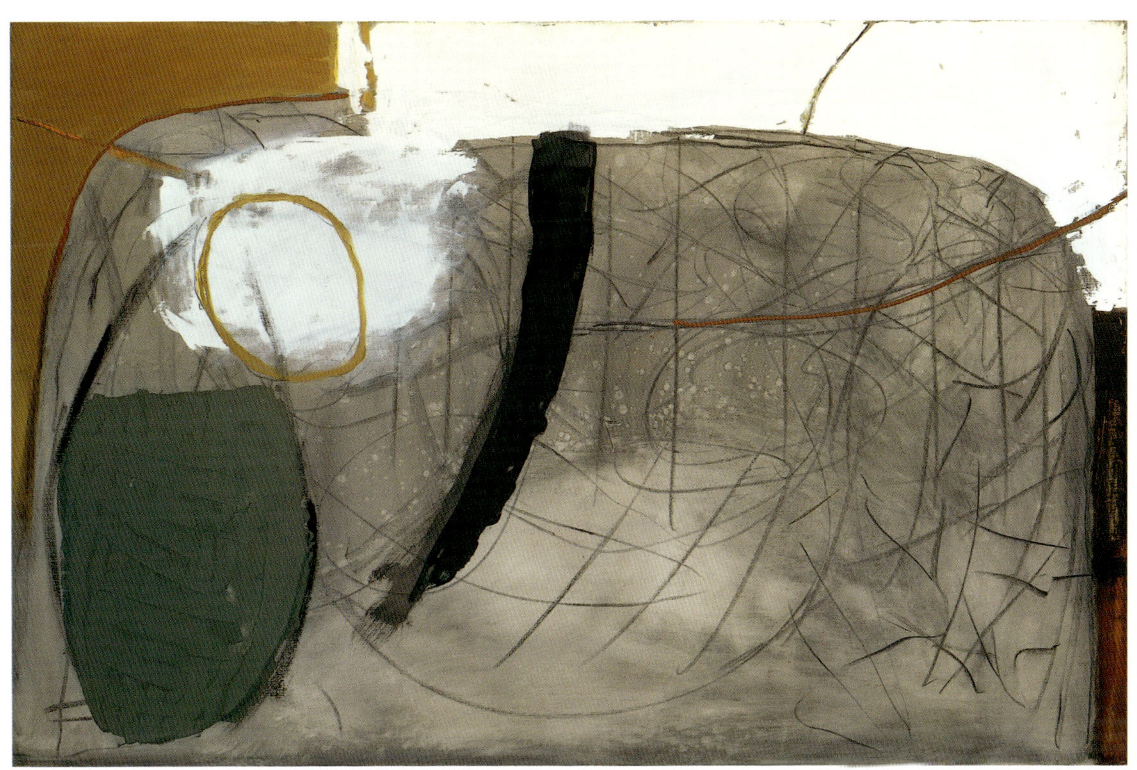

that because established painting techniques had been developed for figurative purposes a new form of expression was needed for a non-figurative art. Instead, he proposed that the fact that past art had been figurative was irrelevant as painting had, in fact, 'been built up … [as] an instrument capable of embodying men's inner truths'.[3] The text is a call once again to embrace paint as medium and, of course, an implicit dismissal of those painters who felt compelled to abandon that practice for construction or architecture. He agreed with Greenberg that modernism's shedding of 'expendable conventions' had liberated the painter to use the full range of technique without fear of falling into past conventions. In what may be a swipe at artists like Pollock, however, he also warned that

In much painting today we are being given paint which is delightful but which has not been put to the sterner but ultimately more rewarding task of presenting something other than itself so that itself becomes transfigured in the process.[4]

The transfiguration of paint had been a key concept for some time. This aspect became more forthright over the following three years.

In 1961, Hilton laid a similar emphasis on the importance of the material and practice of painting. Now, however, he continued the argument that a technique developed for figurative expression could equally be used for non-figurative expression by stating that abstraction was, itself, only a means of shedding the conventions of figuration. To his past colleagues this would have seemed like heresy:

Abstraction has been due not so much to a positive thing but to the absence of a valid image.
Abstraction in itself is nothing. It is only a step towards a new figuration, that is, one which is more true. However beautiful they may be, one can no longer depict women as Titian did. … For an abstract painter there are two ways out or on: he must give up painting and take to architecture, or he must reinvent figuration.[5]

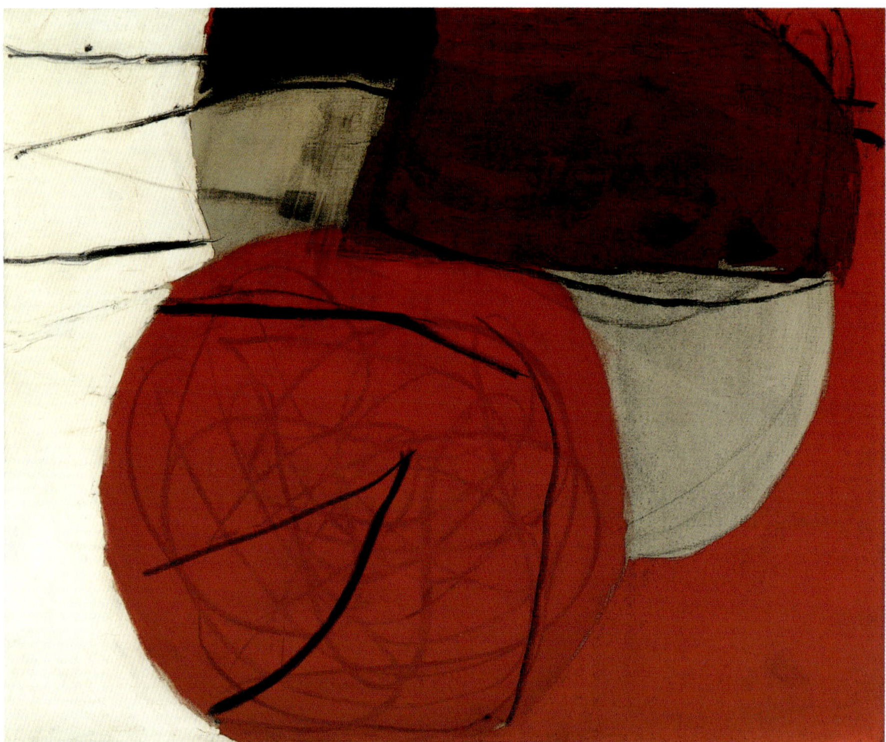

The reinvention of figuration: that is what Hilton seems to have taken on at the end of the 1950s and which, combined with an even more confident command of technique and media, led him to produce such powerful paintings.

It seems to have been in spring 1960 that a clear change in Hilton's work became evident. The paintings he made over the following three years were not overtly figurative, but gradually one comes to find in them something that suggests the human body. It remains difficult to specify exactly what it is that creates that impression. Probably one of the key elements in this suggested – and suggestive – figuration is Hilton's technique itself. It is probably this more than anything that is the most innovative, distinctive and accomplished aspect of these works. *March 1960* (fig.31) is one of the first of this kind of painting, though one might question the term, as it is as much a drawing as a painting. Areas of the canvas are covered with blocks of oil paint: ochre, white, grey, black. The majority of the field, however, is covered only with charcoal marks – long sweeping gestures, short flicks, broader rubbings – some are sharp while many have been rubbed to create a misty, layered effect so that the surface seems like a palimpsest, a document on which successive marks have been repeatedly made and erased. There is no sense of the drawing on the canvas being beneath the painted layer as Hilton would happily draw the charcoal across or through the paint. This subversion of orthodox hierarchies of painting practice, which had first appeared in his work in 1956, is one of the defining characteristics of his painting in the 1960s. These marks and movements across the surface of the picture serve to suggest, subliminally almost, the human body.

Soon after this work, Hilton found a new simplicity. Or rather, he found a means of combining the apparently provisional nature of *March 1960* with the simplicity of the paintings from 1953–4. The result was a body of work of the most extreme economy. Few and simple cursory forms – one or two charcoal lines and a single thick blob of paint, say — could be enough to constitute the most affective and suggestive image. In a series of paintings from 1960 we can see their different aspects. *June 1960* (fig.32) includes two elements that appear in many of the works of 1960–3: blocks of luscious, creamy white oil paint and an informal network of scraggy, wandering charcoal lines, some thick, some thin, some half-erased. Over parts of the image, rich red oil has been painted like a glaze so that the drawing is visible through it. Further drawing has also been applied over and into the red. Such is the allusive nature of the image that the thin and irregular strip of bare canvas towards the bottom between the two areas of red creates a tension that is as much sensual as formal. The same is true in *July 1960* (fig.33), in which a large area of warm chocolatey brown kisses a cool, breast-like oval of white. In another of the same month a compositional tension exists as a result of the gravitational pull between the blue square at the top left with its lines of blue seeming to escape from it and the patch of interweaving short charcoal lines below it. Again, the image is dominated by an area of white oil seen, mostly,

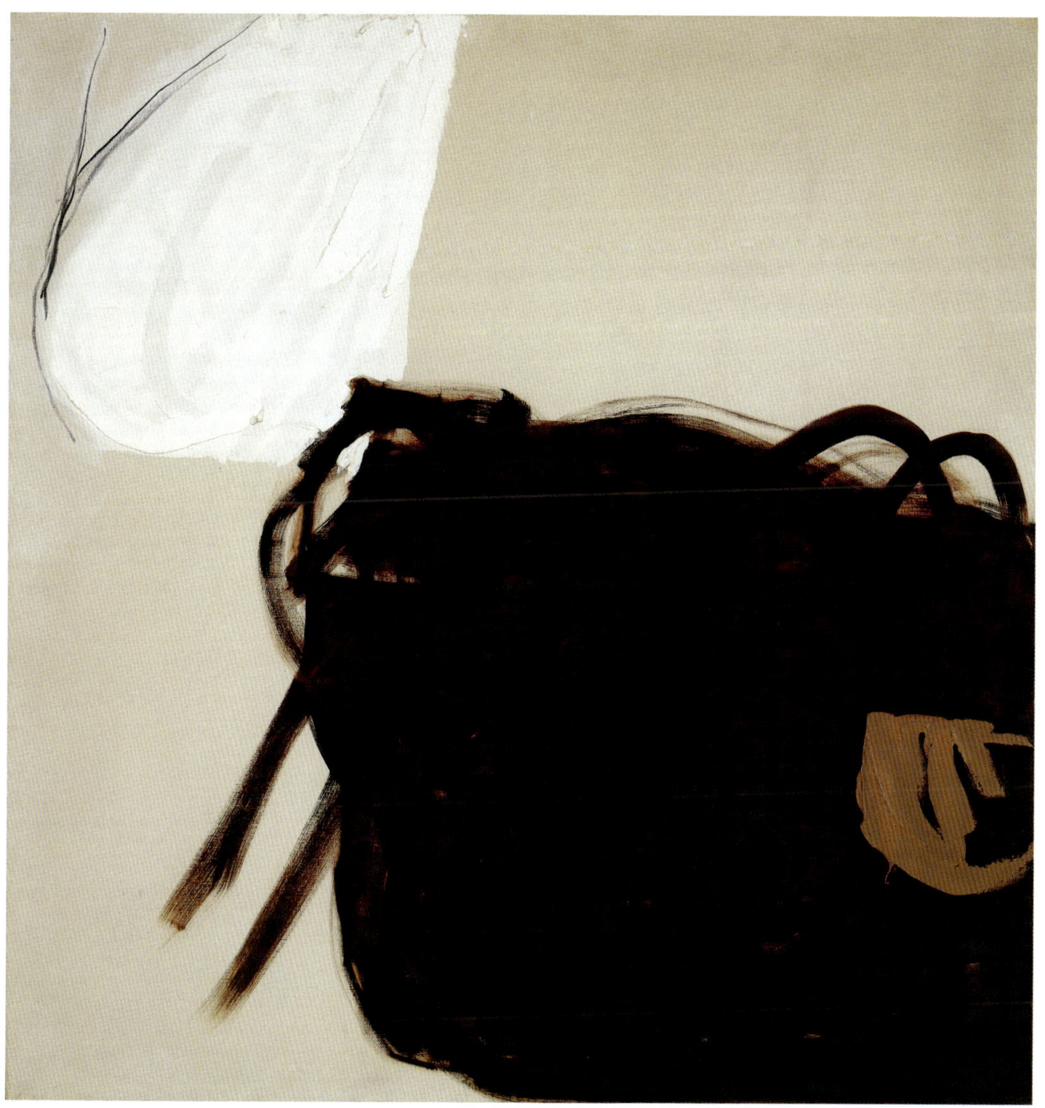

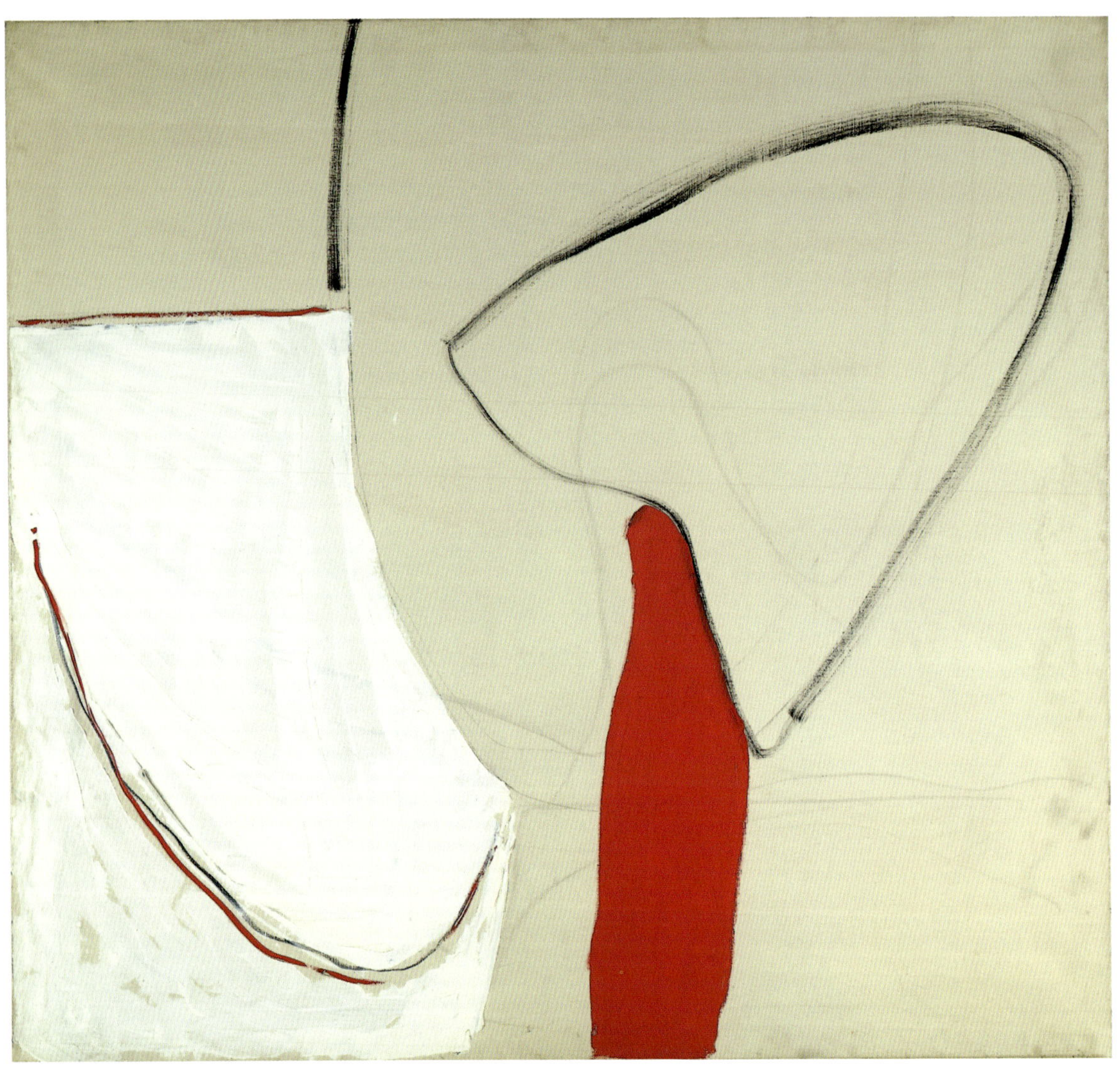

against the darker white of the ground. White on white was an important imple-
ment in Hilton's pictorial tool kit and was almost the only constituent in several
works.

These works seem to suggest the body in a variety of ways, not simply through
form. It is generally an erotic body that seems to be implied or, at least, an excessive or abject body. That is to say that what is suggested is not the contained,
classical nude preferred by high art but a vulgar one defined as much by function
as form. So, suggestions of breasts and buttocks are unsurprisingly common. So
too are phallic symbols − most clearly, perhaps, in the majestic *January 1962*
(fig.35). Possibly the most compelling of this group of works is *February 1961*
(fig.36), which appears to seek to express the idea of a body of fluids and functions. Over, under and around an area of white oil, a strong charcoal line wanders,
apparently aimlessly. As if unconsciously, it describes a form that might be the
cleavage between a pair of breasts or buttocks. It could, equally and paradoxi-
cally, be read as a woman's genitalia or the glans of a penis. At the same time,
ochre paint has been applied in a back and forward gesture as casual as the
working of the charcoal. The effect is as if the image has been smeared with

34
March 1961 1961
Oil and charcoal on
canvas 132 × 140
Private Collection

35
January 1962 (tall white) 1962
Oil and charcoal on
canvas 152.5 × 76
Private Collection

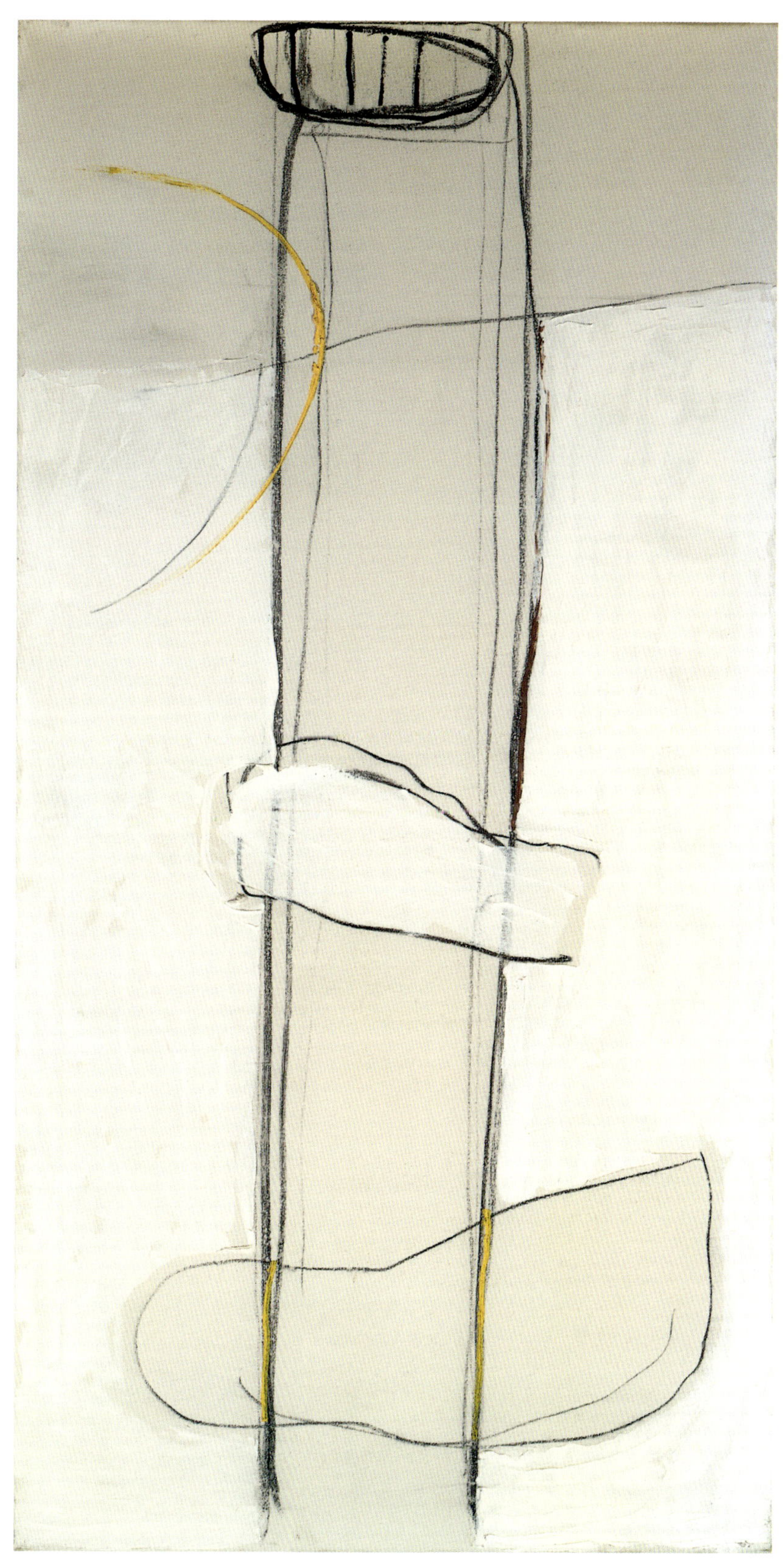

excrement. This, then, is the visceral body understood through its processes. For Hilton, such functions offered a metaphor for the creative process: 'Painting is personal like a shit or a fuck'.[6] Of course, at the same time, one could say that these marks of ochre oil paint function formally as a reassertion of the picture surface. That ambiguity is surely its point.

Hilton's use of white on white is a reminder of the context within which these works were made. By the beginning of the 1960s, he had arrived at a confident position in relation to the development of modernist painting just as the successors to the American Abstract Expressionists became established. On the one hand, painters had reduced their pictures to nothing but monochromatic fields. On the other, they had focused on the flatness of the painting by abandoning traditional painting techniques for pouring and staining. In a caustic exchange with Greenberg, who he considered the only critic good enough to attack, Hilton described Pollock as a 'decorative artist' and set about Morris Louis and other 'fools who stain'. Dismissing Greenberg's nationalism, Hilton argued that the future lay in a fusion of the artistic developments on either side of the Atlantic.[7] Hilton considered that the modernist progression had reached a logical end point and so painting had to return to first principles. 'The mechanism of painting has to be harnessed to some idea', he wrote. 'Now we can expose a totally blank canvas and hardly an eyebrow will be raised. You can't go further than that. So we have to start again and paint something'.[8] That something was, of course, the human figure. In fact, as we have seen, for Hilton, ethically art should either move into architecture or return to the figure. Equally as important as the revived content was the technical aspect. Hilton seems to have accepted Greenberg's theory of modernism as the reduction of each art form, through the shedding of

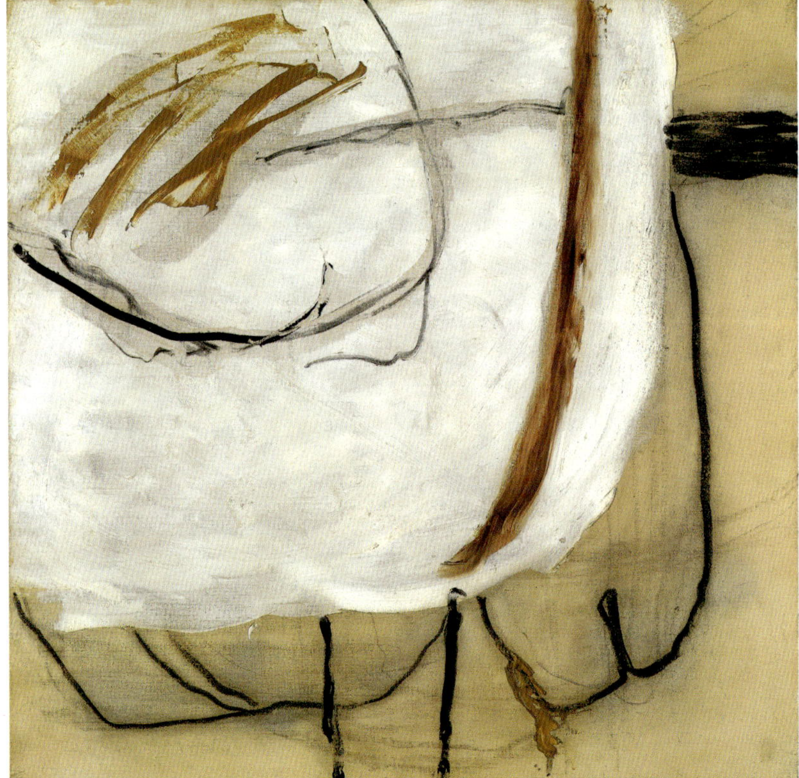

36
February 1961 1961
Oil on canvas 66 × 66

Private Collection

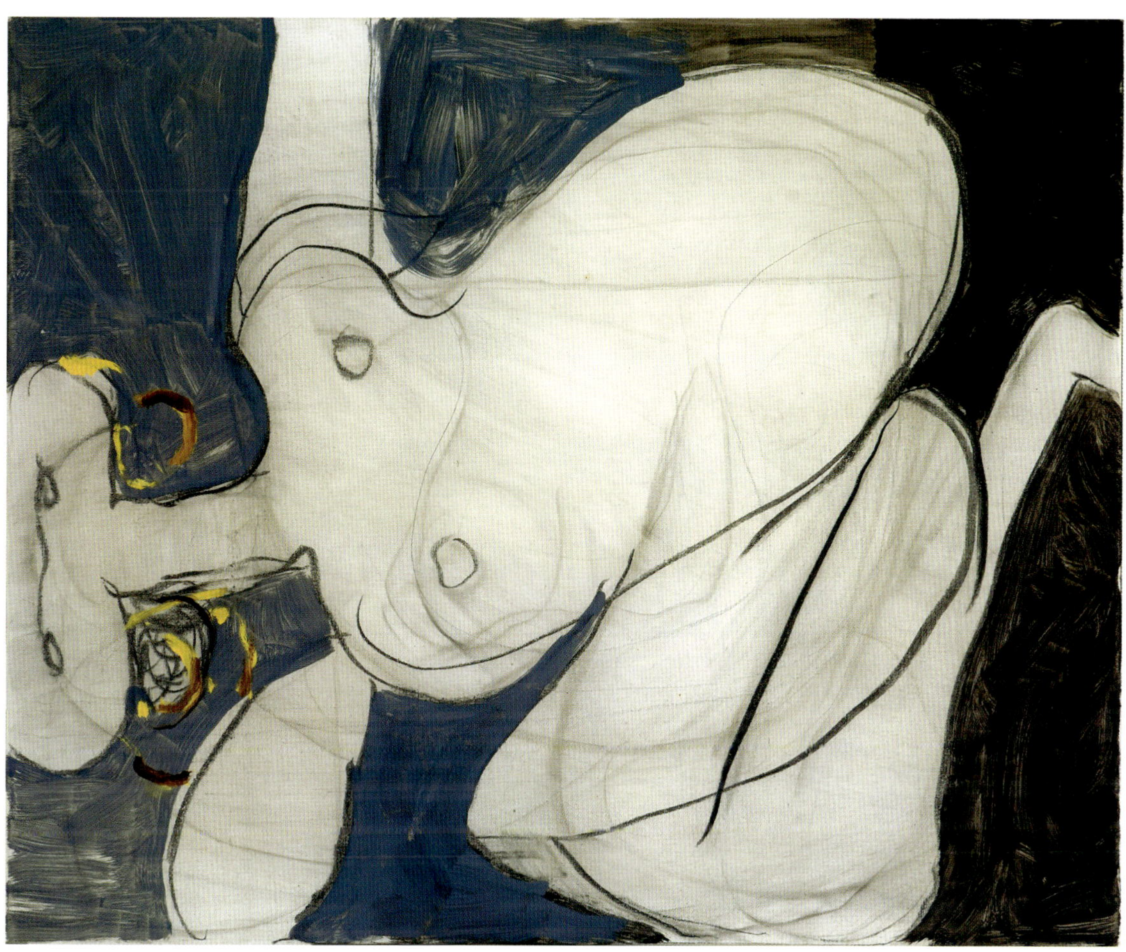

37
Figure 1961 1961
Oil and charcoal on
canvas 76 × 91.5

Southampton City Art
Gallery

'expendable conventions', to those elements that distinguish it from all other forms of expression. For Greenberg, the thing that distinguished painting from every other form of art was flatness; for Hilton, it seems, it was paint itself.

So, a new emphasis on the artist's materials was a riposte to the successors to Abstract Expressionism that Greenberg promoted. The impulsive, impassioned, clearly improvised surfaces of Hilton's paintings, with their graffiti-like pattern of charcoal marks juxtaposed with luscious surfaces of pure oil, are thus clear assertions of the primacy of media. It is important to note that, however much his work was associated by critics with Abstract Expressionism, Hilton was critical of the concept of action painting. In 1957 he wrote a critique of a series of articles by Alloway on action painting. 'I do not like the emphasis on action', he wrote. 'It is ridiculous to see more action in one type of work than another. The activity is always mental.' So he insisted that all art is the result of a primarily cerebral process, a series of conscious decisions, even if the end result is intended to look as if it were the product of some unconscious act.[9] There is some contradiction here, possibly. Hilton was dismissive of the idea of 'composition', suggesting that a picture should be more improvised than such an organisation would suggest.[10] To put primary emphasis on the mental process while dismissing such premeditation would seem to assign a key role to subconscious mental processes as opposed simply to the physical action that results.

Hilton approved of Alloway's use of the term 'existential' in this context,   53 'despite this being a portmanteau word'.[11] He wrote of the artist being nothing more than an intermediary between a 'philosophical standpoint' and the act of expressing it in paint. In an existentialist vein: there is a sense in which the emphasis on materials and gesture serve to highlight the artist and the process of each work's manufacture. The apparent simplicity and immediacy of the images make the viewer all the more conscious of their maker and the process by which they came to exist. More than that, the emphasis on the layers of half-erased charcoal that results in a kind of web of allusive marks demonstrates the painting to be contingent and provisional, open to further change and development. It is as if we see a work in progress, defying the more orthodox sense that a work of art has an inevitable finished state that the artist is striving to find or reveal. Somehow, this suggested temporality of the works of art brings the artist to the fore, so that the works and the marks of which they are made become like records of their maker's passing. One is reminded of Francis Bacon's idea of painting being like a snail's trail of slime – a record that one had passed through. The critic Pierre Rouve highlighted this aspect of Hilton's idea, suggesting that Hilton's art was a constant act of 'self-creation', achieving what the artist called a 'complete wholeness' that Rouve equated with Heidegger's *Darsein* (being in the world).[12]

There is a sense that when Hilton spoke of humanising painting now that the modernist progression had reached its logical extreme he had in mind this re-affirmation of the subjectivity of the artist. It was principally, however, through the representation of the human figure that he saw this humanising taking place. In *Figure 1961* (fig.37), for the first time in years, he made a painting which is unambiguously figurative. At the same time, it is completely consistent with the works of that period in which the figurative is more implicit. The figure is shown distorted, on her side, her head squashed to fit into the frame, one arm raised, the other so truncated that one is not sure if it is arm or breast that reaches down to the bottom edge of the canvas. Bodily details are suggested with the barest possible means: two nipples, two eyes and some curls of yellow paint for hair. Again, as in *March 1960* (fig.31), apparently random swirls of semi-erased charcoal appear to underlie the paint and serve to define the surface of the body without creating the illusion of depth. It is as if a body's skin were articulated by a caressing touch across its surface.

For years Hilton had employed forms that could be read as fragments of the female body. Even in the austere works of 1953–4, allusions to the head or a breast might arguably be identified. *October 1961*, in drawing together such fragments into an unambiguous female figure, seems to confirm such readings. Despite the significance of the departure that this work marked, it did not initially unleash a series of overtly figurative works. Its obvious successors came over two years later in the shape of *Oi Yoi Yoi* (fig.38) and *Dancing Woman*, (fig.39) both from December 1963 and the only instances of Hilton reworking the same idea. These two works are the most wonderfully brazen, crude, excessive nudes. Unquestionably, the female form is opened up for consumption by the male gaze. In both paintings, the subject's legs are raised in opposing directions, her arms outstretched, one breast is viewed front-on while the other is seen in profile bouncing in mid air. The figure's pubic triangle provides the centre point of the canvas. Like that in *Figure 1961* the body's skin is implied and implicitly caressed by the charcoal lines that swoop and turn across the surface. It is difficult to say that these females are simply objectified, however. Unlike that from 1961, which is turned on her side and so confined by the canvas that her head has been

38
Oi Yoi Yoi, December 1963 1963
Oil and charcoal on canvas 152.5 × 127

Tate

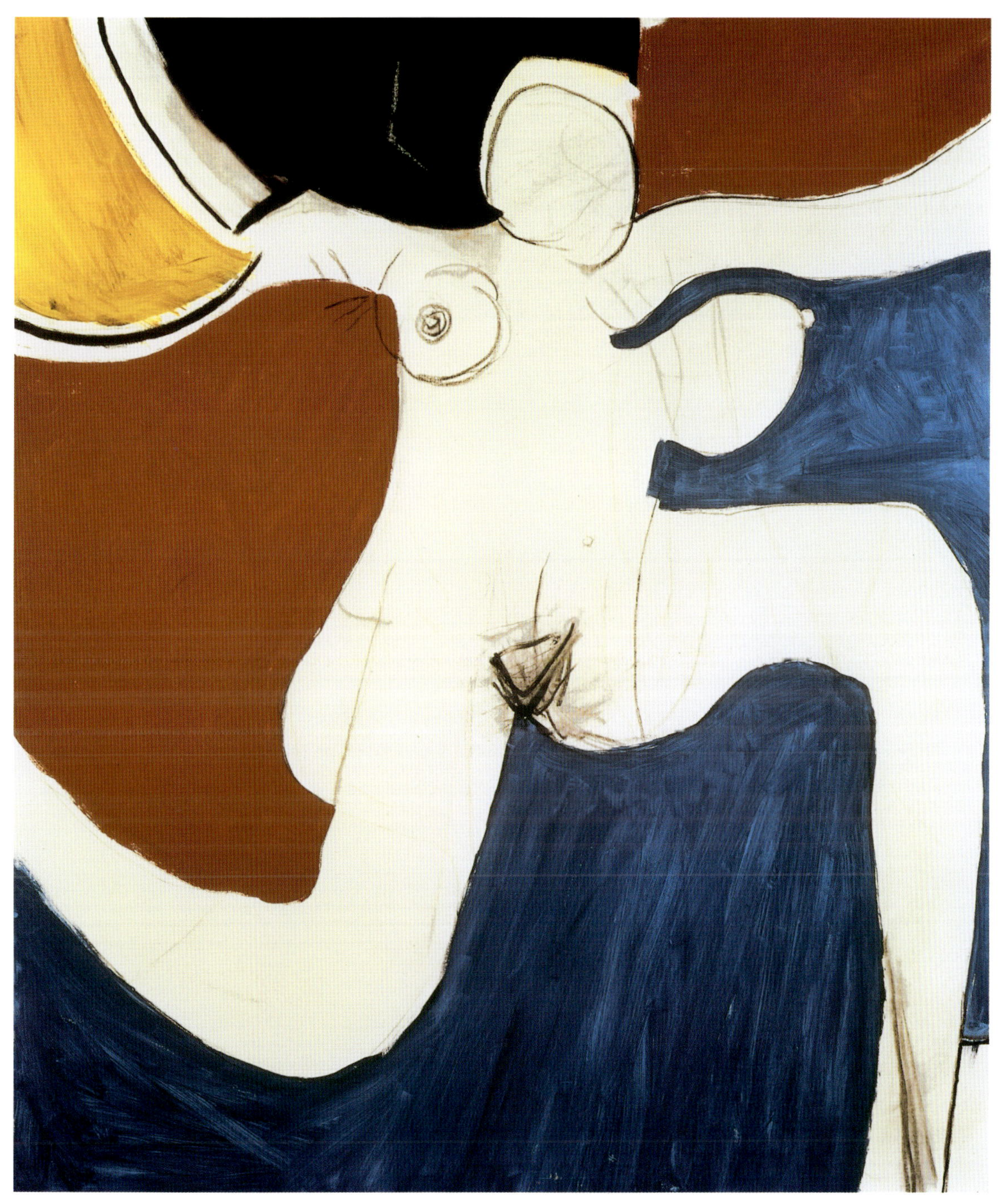

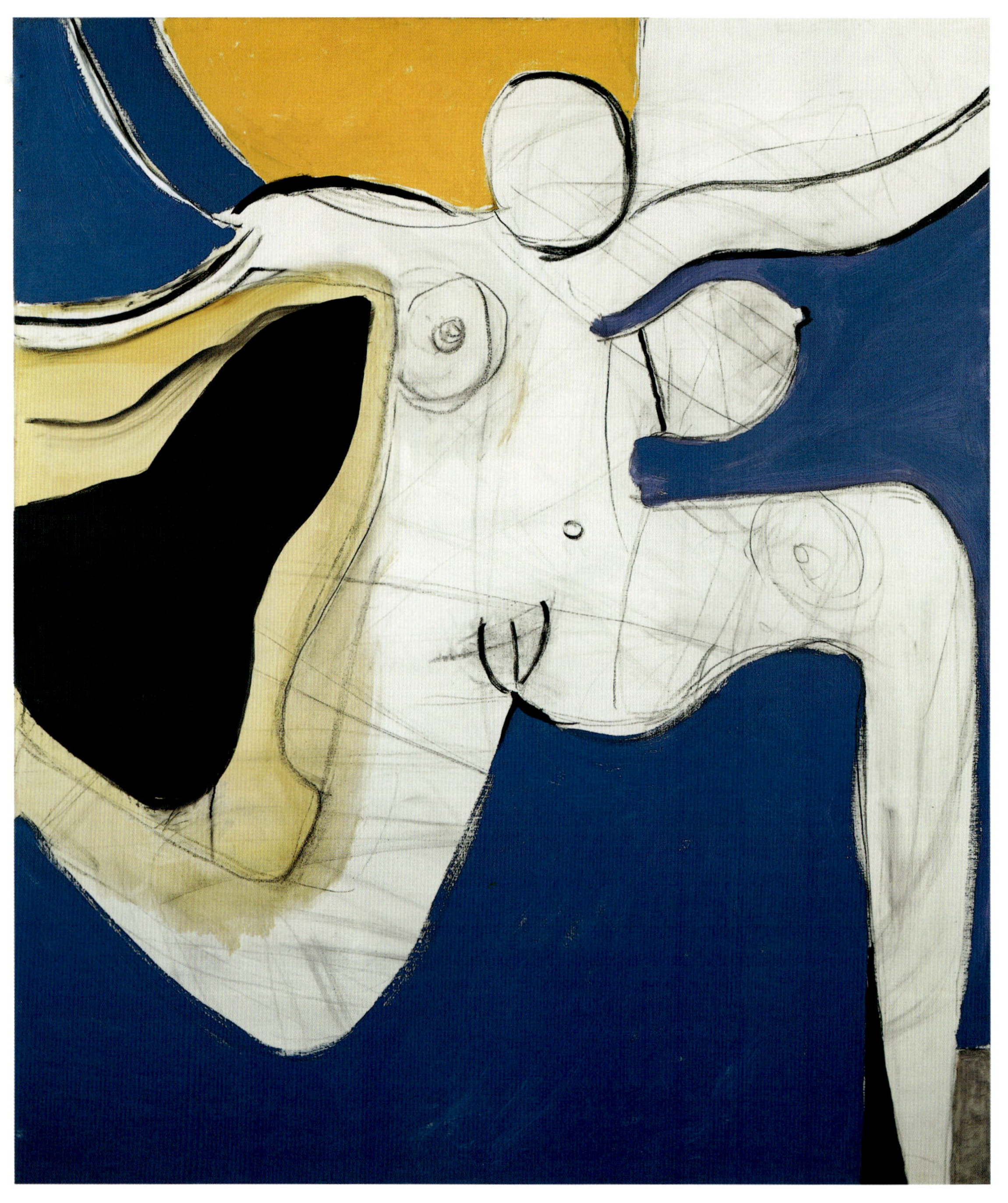

39
Dancing Woman,
December 1963 1963
Oil and charcoal on
canvas 152.5 × 127

Scottish National Gallery of
Modern Art, Edinburgh

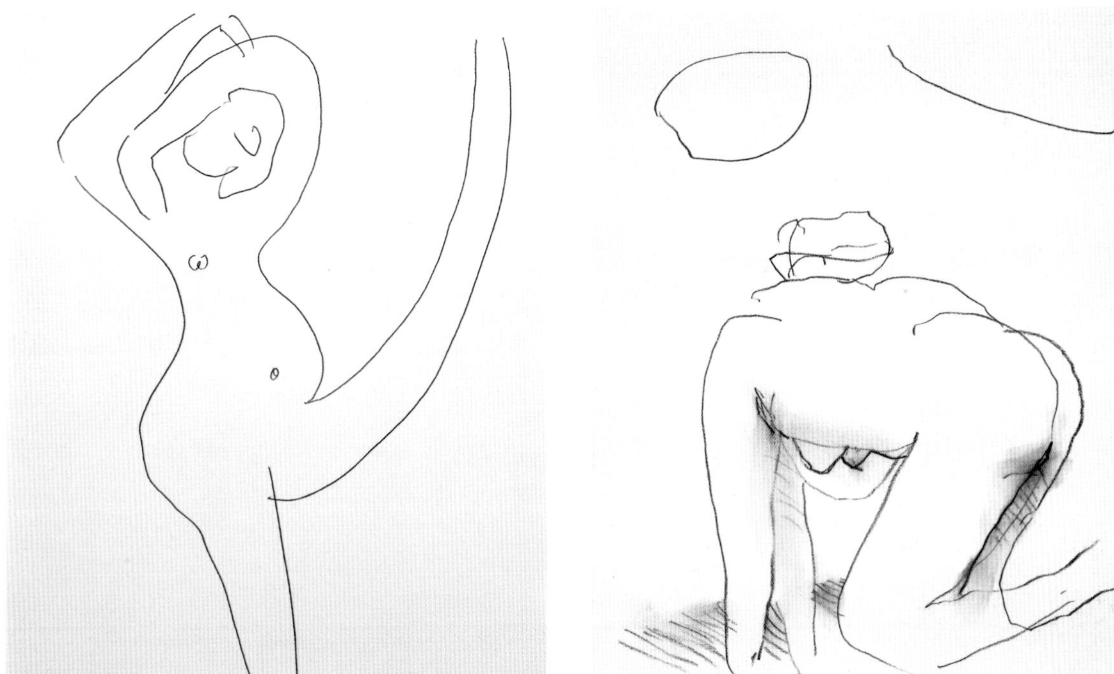

40
Nude early 1960s
Pencil on paper
25.5 × 20.5
Lord Gowrie

41
Nude 1962
Pencil on paper
27 × 21
The British Museum

distorted, here the women seem to dance in freedom and defiance. Undoubtedly they are shown as the objects of erotic fantasy and desire but that does not mean they are simply passive. This is, it might be suggested, the new confident, open body of the 1960s.

Hilton had always drawn the human figure and almost always the female form. His drawings, with their confident, continuous outlines and total absence of shading or modelling show an extraordinary facility at capturing characteristic poses or attitudes with the most minimal of means. In this sense, he drew like Picasso, able to make a figure moving in space believable with only two or three simple lines. While many of his works restrict themselves to fairly conventional poses and others set the figure in slightly comic situations, a majority are injected with an erotic overtone. Inevitably, the manner of representation and the tone of the treatment cast the figure in a passive role as object. This is shown most clearly in one of Hilton's most powerful, eloquent and unsettling drawings. With a few rapidly drawn lines a woman is shown on her hands and knees, viewed almost from her backside (see fig.41). Despite the simplicity of the depiction, the figure, the spatial relations of her constituent parts and an idea of a spatial setting are all believable. Her sex has been blurred where the pencil line has been rubbed – by the artist's thumb perhaps – so that it is both obscured and highlighted for our attention. Whatever the reason for the woman to be on all-fours, it is a position that casts her in a subordinate role. The drawing has an obvious erotic charge suggesting that her pose is sexually driven, the term 'doggy-fashion' that it brings to mind emphasising the objectification that is taking place.

Much has been written about the ways in which the convention of the nude in art has served to objectify and so subjugate women. There is a sense in which Hilton, through the brazen nature and honest eroticism of his representation, tackles the issue head-on and makes it overt. One can undoubtedly find a misogynistic dimension to his depictions of the female form and in his attitude to

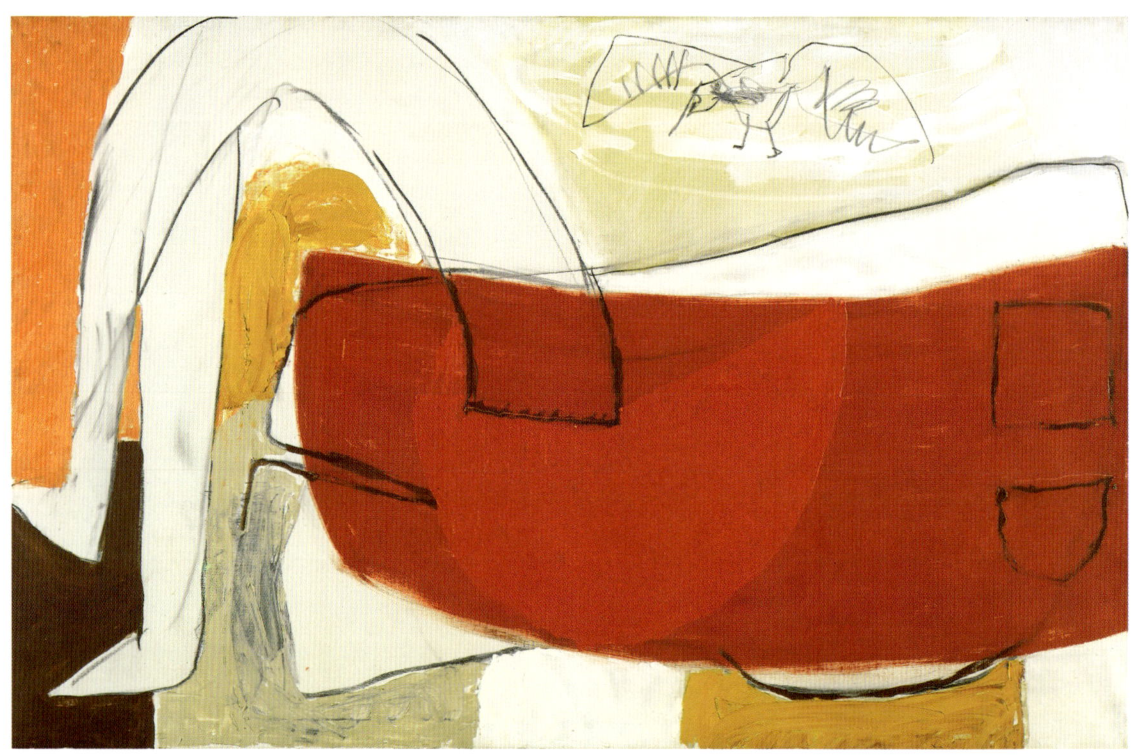

women more broadly. There is in addition, however, a tenderness in the close observation that underpins his drawings of bodies in motion. Thousands of line drawings show women standing in different settings, reclining, bending over, seated, knees raised and seen from above as if in the bath. In many drawings the obvious everyday situations in which the figures have been observed add to their erotic charge as they can seem to possess the power of voyeurism. There are also drawings which are almost non-representational, but the few arcing lines from which they are made irresistibly compose themselves into views of the female body or, as in one untitled work of the late 1960s, into what appears to be a rear view of a bending body about to be penetrated.

Such sexually charged objectification also found its way into Hilton's painting. In contrast to the unfettered joy of the dancing figure in *Oi Yoi Yoi*, that in the slightly earlier *Figure and Bird* (fig.42) seems more vulnerable and threatened. In this work, the woman, stretched out and laid bare, becomes a landscape. Woman as metaphor for landscape is a common trope used by artists such as Peter Lanyon. Here, the landscape is identified as a female body by two breasts and an indented linear form denoting the vagina. While the arching, and apparently crossed, legs light-heartedly inject a sense of the everyday, the highlighting of the sexual organs casts the body as an image of eroticism and fecundity. The latter is further emphasised by the hotter red area within the main part of the body that may suggest a womb-like inner core. A similar fusion of the fertile female body and the land appears in *January 1964* (fig.43). The form of this work is derived from a late Bill Brandt photograph in which a woman's hips are seen close-up so that her body becomes like a hill echoing the landscape beyond. *January 1964* seems more clearly concerned with the idea of woman and land as nurturing and generative forces. In *Figure and Bird*, however, a sexual tension seems present as the scraggy bird flies over or, perhaps, comes into land on the

42
*Figure and Bird,
September 1963* 1963
Oil and charcoal on
canvas 117 × 178

Southampton City Art
Gallery

43
January 1964 (red)
1964
Oil and charcoal on
canvas 126.9 × 152.4

Arts Council Collection

prone body. Some have suggested the image might be read as 'an earth-bound body visited by an enlivening, or life-conceiving spirit'.[13] One might contend, however, that the bird seems more predatory than that, perhaps priapic. The painting then becomes one of sexual fantasy as the scrawny male bird looks down upon the exposed and vulnerable body.

These landscape works have been connected to Hilton's association with Cornwall, but it was only in late 1965 that he and his family decided to move there permanently. By the time they moved to a small cottage in Botallack, close to the sea cliffs near St Just, Hilton had married Rose Phipps and their eldest son, Bo, was four and the youngest, Fergus, just born. By that stage Hilton was well established, having won First Prize at the John Moores competition in 1963 and represented Britain at the Venice Biennale the following year. His influence on such younger artists as the Australian Brett Whiteley was widely acknowledged. Despite or because of these successes, Hilton's behaviour was increasingly erratic. His drunken conduct at the John Moores awards dinner received unfortunate press attention, as the husband of a famous member of parliament had a heart attack during the meal and died shortly afterwards. As early as the 1950s, Hilton had told Frost he was 'on the primrose path to destruction' and this seemed to be the case.[14]

The move to Cornwall seems to have exacerbated the situation. The boundaries between work, home and recreation broke down. His studio was in the house at Botallack and there was a social circle, in particular the poet Sydney Graham, ready to join in drinking sessions. There was, it seems, a certain mad-

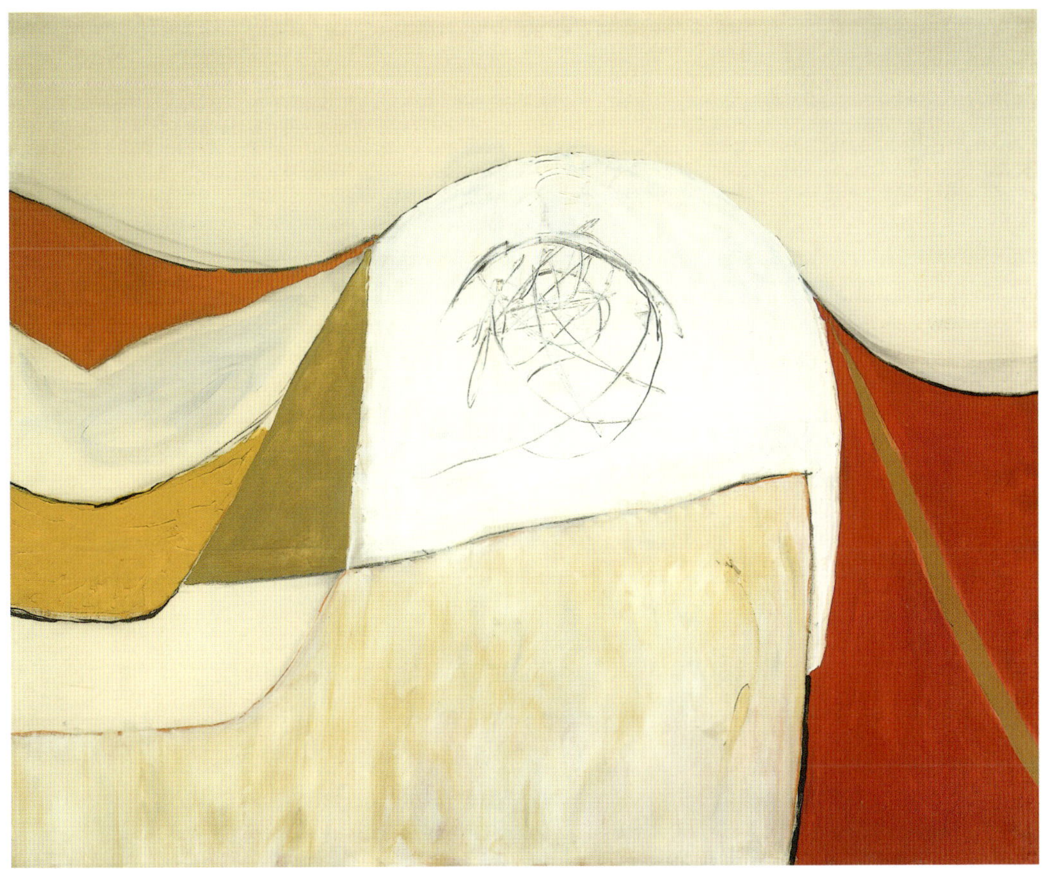

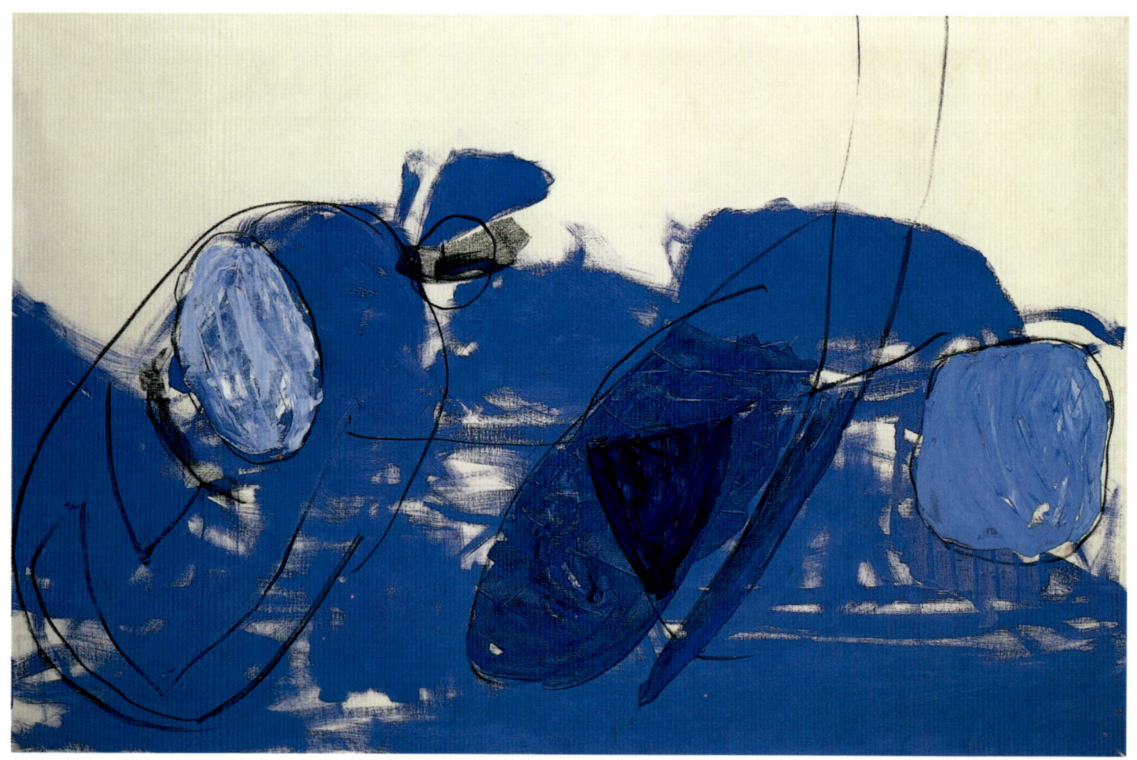

ness to the life of the following few years. In 1966 Hilton spent six weeks in Exeter gaol after his third drink-driving offence and only escaped a longer sentence by agreeing to undergo treatment at St Lawrence's Hospital, Bodmin. In 1968, he spent time drying out at the Priory Clinic, Roehampton; he seemed to be happy to be sober but, having left the hospital to receive his CBE from the Queen, shortly after leaving Buckingham Palace he slipped into a pub and off the wagon.

Inevitably, perhaps, the paintings from the second half of the 1960s are less consistent. No doubt Hilton's physical situation was a key factor. However, it also appears that his perennial concerns about the way forward for painting continued. When first in Cornwall, he wrote to Terry Frost, 'What to paint when I get my studio I haven't a clue'.[15] What's more, having apparently found a means of expression that could be either figurative or abstract, he wrote again to Frost from Cornwall, 'It is a terrible thing to have to admit that the time is not yet come for figuration in painting. My efforts in that direction make me sick'.[16] So Hilton continued to produce a mixture of suggestive figurative paintings alongside totally non-representational works. He proved by practice that the two could be interchangeable. Reviewing his exhibition at Waddington's in 1971 – six years after the last – Norbert Lynton declared that 'those who keep on announcing the death of painting … should have a look at Hilton', and insisted that he had achieved unique success even among those painters who had fundamentally tested their medium. The reason, he seemed to suggest, was that 'no two Hiltons are alike', the showing including a wide range of work from totally abstract to external references, with a variety of marks and techniques. The works, he wrote, were 'held together only by personality, not at all by style or habit.'[17]

The works of this period certainly vary. One group seem to have become much flatter in their surface quality and harder-edged in their forms. Others show overt subject matter – boats, for example, or horses. Some of the last – he abandoned

44
March 1963 1963
Oil and charcoal on
canvas 101.6 × 177.8

Walker Art Gallery, National
Museums Liverpool

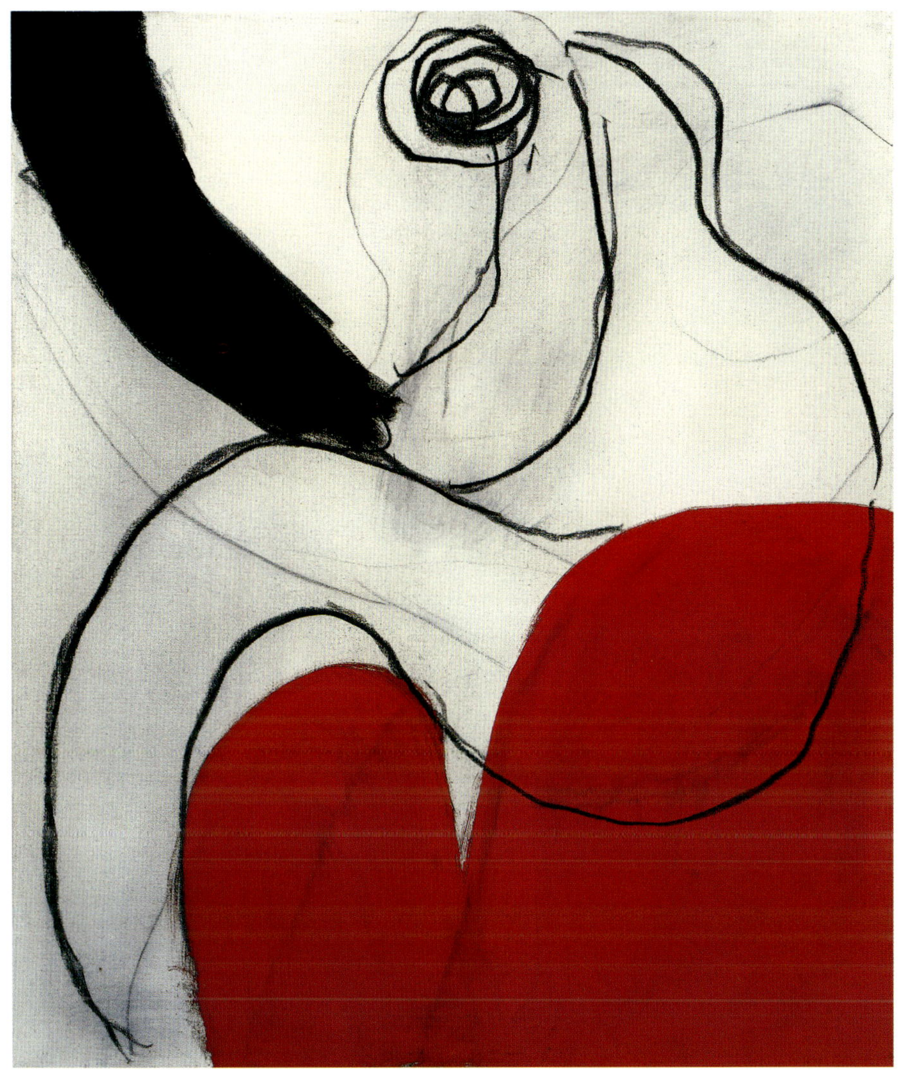

oil paint in 1972 — could seem stiff and unresolved. A work like *Untitled 1971* (fig.46) seems to veer to the other extreme, being an uninhibited frenzy of brightly coloured shapes, having no obvious external reference. It is, it seems, simply a Dionysian outburst of pleasure. Nevertheless, the most successful works of the late 1960s are those closest in manner to the work of the early sixties. In *May 1968* (fig.45), for instance, one long, curving charcoal line describes the female body from the back of her neck to her ankle, another the front of her leg, two more her arm and a spiral of charcoal defines her bowed head. With two areas of colour, one black and one red, this is enough to provide an image that not only represents a seated female figure but communicates something of personality or, better perhaps, of the character that provides her humanity. With the most economic of means, Hilton thus created an image of great passion and humanity.

During the 1960s, despite awesome personal challenges, Hilton produced one of the most sophisticated manifestations of late modernist painting. After much experimentation, he managed to find a language in which he could paint both figuratively and abstractly. The key binding characteristic was a practice that rejected any idea of convention and hierarchy, a form of painting in which char-

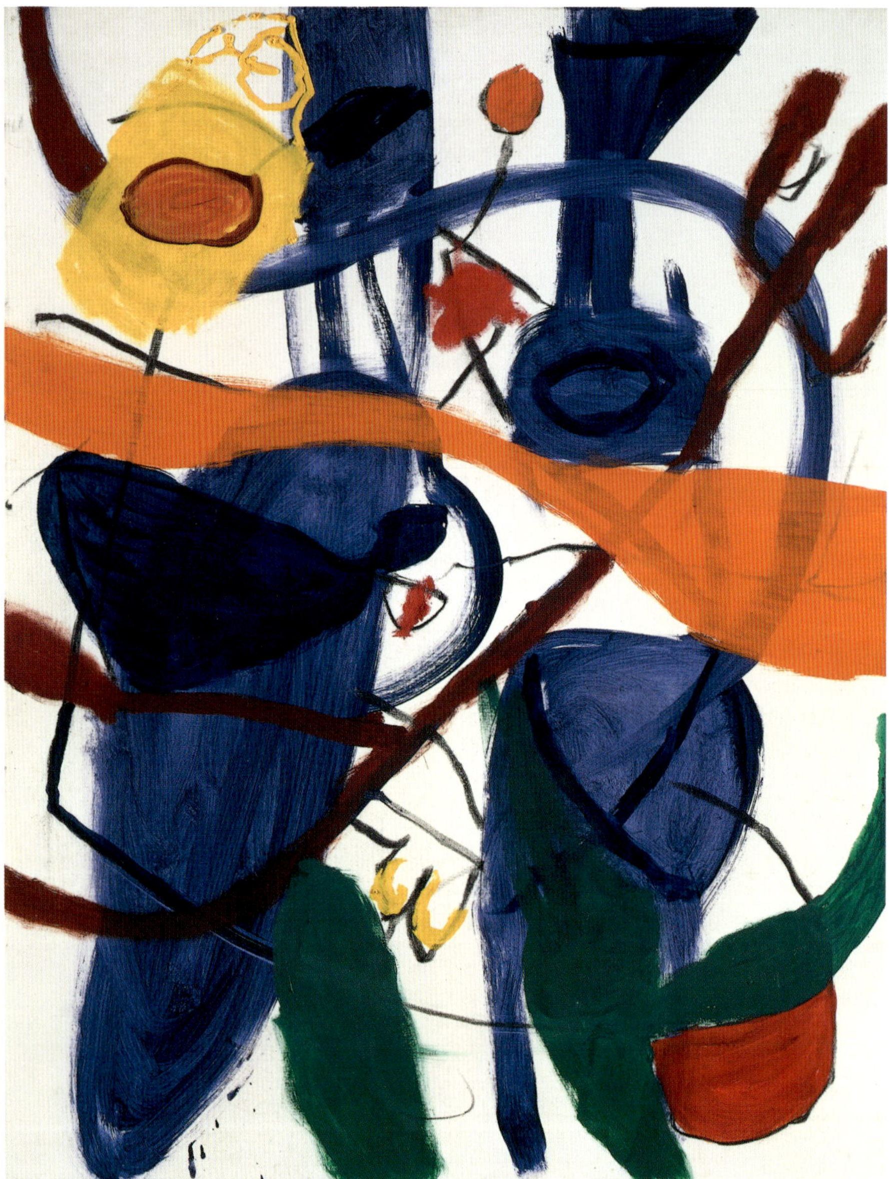

coal drawing could have equal authority as oil paint. Contrary to Greenberg's insistence on European artists' fatal retention of traditional aesthetic values, Hilton brought a crude vulgarity to painting that made the Americans look polite, if not pretty. Against their fields of colour or networks of lacy dribbles he proffered a wide range of materials and handling that embodied a humanism through their very lively, brash and crude nature. As in life, Hilton obeyed no conventions of politeness or correct behaviour but, instead, held a mirror up to contemporary painting. More than anything, the injection into modernist practice of a crude vulgarity and visceral corporeality relates Hilton to Picasso. There are few comparisons among his contemporaries, however. Dubuffet's raw figures offer one parallel, Philip Guston's rejection of abstraction for a cartoon-like figuration another. In 1972, Hilton's art underwent a change of an equally dramatic nature.

47
Untitled 1973
Gouache on paper
30.5 × 47.6

Lord Gowrie

By the beginning of the 1970s, Hilton's production had reduced greatly. One listing records as few as seven oils completed in 1969, eleven in 1970, eight in 1971 and seven in 1972.[1] In late 1972, however, he embarked upon what would turn out to be one of the most extraordinary bodies of late work by any artist of the twentieth century. Between October that year and his death in February 1975, Hilton produced hundreds of works in gouache on paper. In these, even more than before, the human figure, suggestions of narrative and a wry sense of humour asserted their presence. To some, these small paintings might have seemed like an anomaly, something distinct from his earlier work and less significant, forced upon him by circumstances. In fact, one might view them as another stage in Hilton's negotiations between abstraction and representation and between the technical and human dimensions of art production. As such, they should be taken seriously as the final phase in his artistic career.

To separate these works off from Hilton's personal circumstances is especially difficult. He suffered from peripheral neuritis, the first consequence of which was

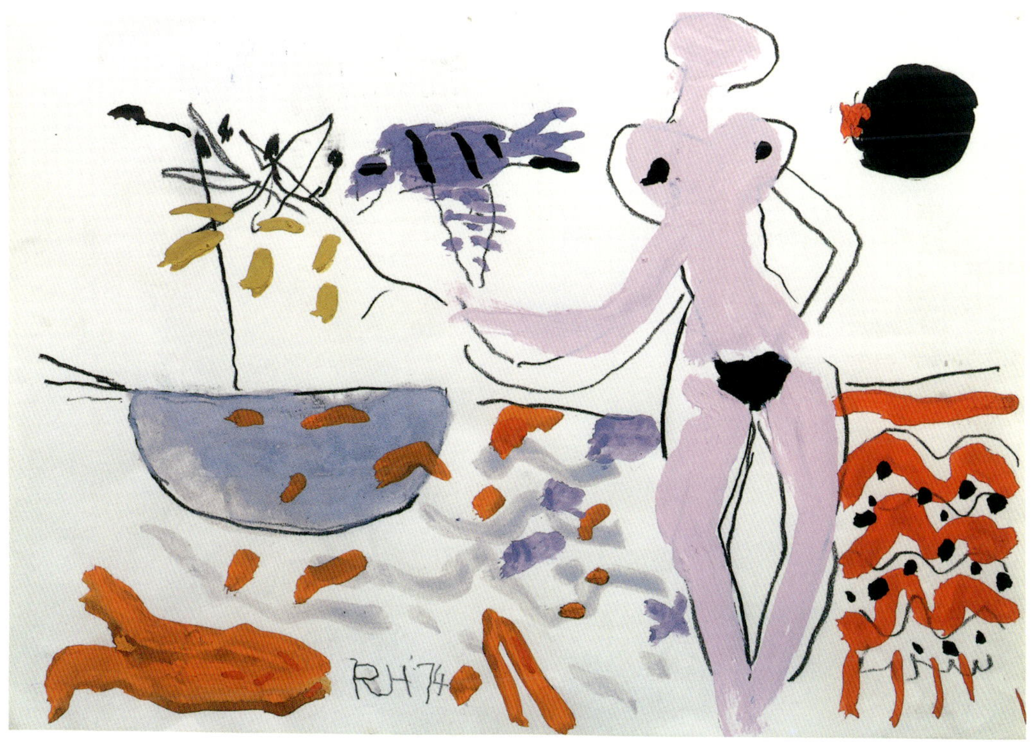

a loss of mobility, meaning that from October 1972 he could no longer reach his upstairs studio and was forced to work in the bedroom below. He also suffered a skin condition that caused incessant irritation and great discomfort. As the artist himself recorded in a letter to the editor of *Studio International*, Peter Townsend:

I have largely lost the use of my legs, the arms & midriff are going. I have a skin condition which is driving me mad. All this is caused by alcohol. The usual vicious circle. You have to have more to cover up the pain which it creates. I say this to show how, being bed-ridden, I fell back on gouaches.[2]

As he suggests, these works owe their physical characteristics to practical considerations. Confined to bed, he could not use oils as he had before. It is said that his move into gouache – or more precisely poster paint – was stimulated by the gift of a pack of such paints to his son for Christmas 1972. Such children's colours, along with to a lesser extent pen and ink, crayon, charcoal and pencil, were the raw materials for Hilton's last years. Any child-like quality that the works might gain from the paint is exaggerated by the ways in which Hilton was forced to make them. Though some photographs show him sitting on his bed with his painting on a low table or the floor between his legs, many others show him reclining on one side. His skin affliction obliged him to rest on his left elbow. As he was left-handed he was forced to paint with his 'wrong' hand. This lent the works a wobbly cack-handedness akin to that found in children's drawings.

Despite the conditions under which these new paintings were made, Hilton continued to pay close attention to technical considerations. He was also quick to assign new aesthetic parameters to his enforced change of medium. The works themselves are modest in size but nearly always boldly coloured. Paint has never been mixed on the paper, so the colours have a strength and intensity that animate the image. In some, the design was drawn before painting; in others, paint seems to have been applied straight on to blank paper. A number appear to be completely non-representational but the majority are figurative, depicting animals, human figures and even what appear to be specific narratives. Some show dwellings, actual or imagined. Despite all this, Hilton managed to maintain his commitment to the integrity of the picture surface. Though environments and contexts are frequently suggested he does not create the illusion of recessive or pictorial space. The bald mattness of the pigment, the stark white of the paper and this flatness of the image can give the paintings an almost iconic appearance. At the same time, each paint-mark displays the same degree of energy as Hilton's handling of oil had done in the past. Similarly, he applies the

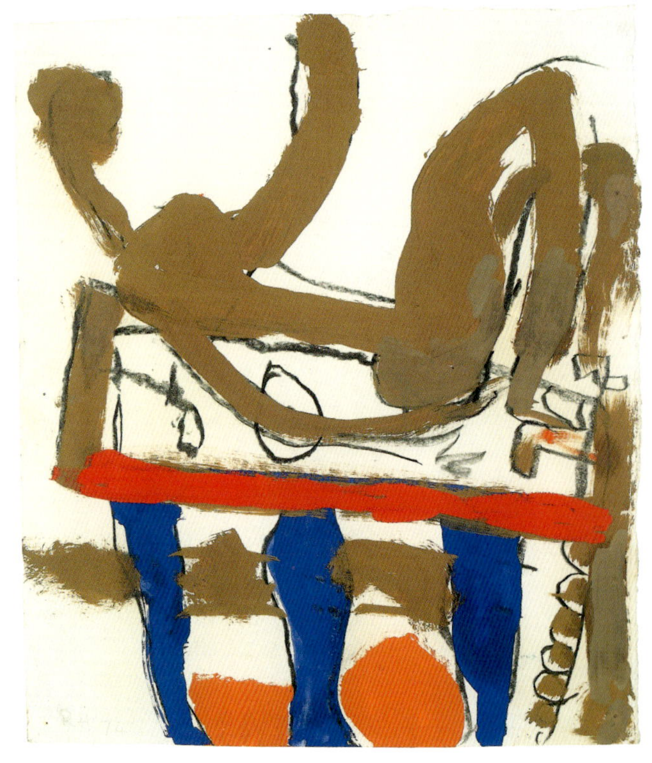

48
Untitled 1974
Gouache and charcoal
on paper 50.8 × 42.5

Sheffield City Art Gallery

49
Untitled 1974
Gouache and charcoal
on paper 19 × 27.9

Private Collection

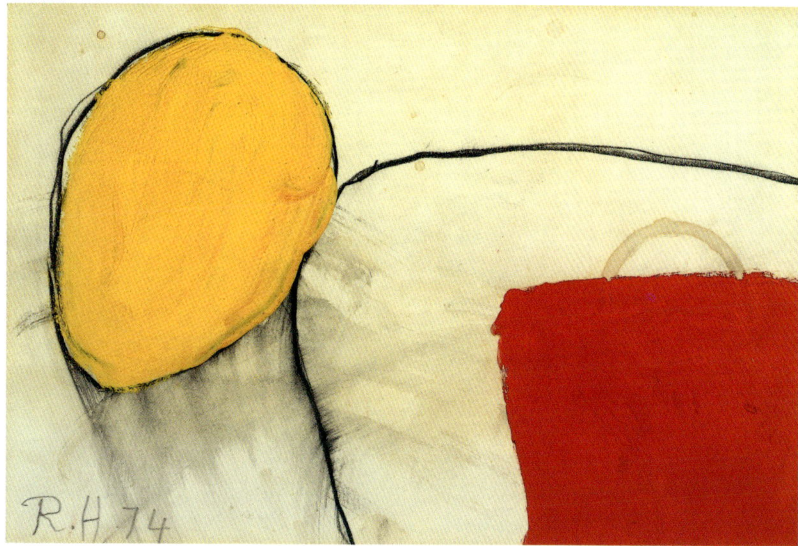

poster colour with the confident fluency of his line drawing. It is, perhaps, this quality that can make the occasional work seem slight, as they appear to have been made with the speed of a doodle. The instinctive command of composition, colour and movement raise most of them above such lesser images, however. So too do the typically precise observation and subtle and poignant symbolic imagery.

Hilton was clearly stimulated by the works, if not entirely certain about them. In March 1974, he reported that for nearly eighteen months he had been producing between three and five a day. He wrote to Peter Townsend:

If I have done anything recently, i.e. since Dec. '72, which is any good, it is partly because I have been struggling with a new medium (to me). I find it exciting for 2 reasons

a It is cheap
b It is convenient, i.e. it dries quick & allows superimposing
c I can do it from bed
d The products, once made, can be rapidly disposed of.[3]

He also set out a number of principles that he specifically linked to poster paints, though the list clearly digressed into more general comments about painting – including references to his old lessons from Bissière – and, indeed, about life:

1 Never rub out or attempt to erase; Work round it if you have made a mistake. Make your mistakes a strength rather than a weakness
2 Wait for it. i.e. if you don't get a clear message, do nothing
3 If you have a full brush & you have made a mark do not think you have to use the paint on your brush, wash it out.
4 As in life it is not so much what you put in but what you leave out that counts …
5 Paint as if you were painting a wall. (Bissière)
6 No colour stands alone. They are all influenced by each other. This is where the dicey part comes in. I mean the balancing act. Spilt milk & Mexican corn & a bit of egg & you've got to make something of it.
7 Most pictures can be pulled round. If you run into head winds, tear it up.
8 Don't drink & smoke so much & lay off the nudes. Nice, but too easy a gambit.[4]

Nevertheless, the medium had its disadvantages. Poster paints, Hilton wrote, are naturally inert and to overcome this he initially employed what he described as an 'almost pointillist' style, the Seurat-like technique creating a more energetic paint surface. By March 1974, however, he had 'reached a stage now of simplifying. While I have my food, things get dropped on the paper. Milk bottles upset, spaghetti, sweet corn, cats; it remains to tidy up the mess, which I do with a few simple strokes.'[5] It sounds as if in the paintings was found the simplicity that was so clearly lacking in the circumstances of their making.

The question of the relationship between these works and naive and children's art is important. Hilton, himself, seemed keen to distance his practice from that of children. 'One has to face the eternal problem about children's art', he wrote. 'It is often charming and you can borrow from it. The difference is, I think, that children are essentially realists, whereas a mature painter is not.'[6] Hilton's statement seems counter-intuitive and may well have been intended to make the reader pull themselves up short. It is a common trope in modernism for artists to aspire to the innocence of vision of the child, to escape the conventions derived from their own education and experience. This was recommended by Matisse, whose own late flourish bears obvious comparison with Hilton's. It was also the quality that attracted artists to the artefacts of early and non-western civilisations and to the work of such self-taught artists as Henri Rousseau and, closer to home, Alfred Wallis. Among St Ives artists, Wallis was little short of a cult figure, his works exchanged like talismans. In 1974 Hilton cited both Rousseau and Wallis among the artists to whom he considered himself related (others included 'Miró, Calder, Dufy and of course Matisse') and he owned a small Wallis painting himself.[7] Nevertheless, Hilton's comment on children's art makes an important distinction. Whatever the emphasis he placed on natural talent, and however spontaneous his work had at times seemed, he still placed most value on the conscious decisions made by the painter in the studio. Even these small gouaches, whose eccentricities seem sometimes to echo the rambling conversation of the drunk, are the products of a sequence of deliberations, decisions and conscious physical acts.

It is, similarly, a little unclear what status Hilton put on these works. Not all his informed visitors recognised them as works of art on a par with his earlier paintings and this view may be endorsed by the way he occasionally invited visitors to help themselves.[8] That the content of a number of them is personal, perhaps autobiographical, would support the idea that they were not made with their public dissemination as the primary goal. John Miller, who framed some of the earlier gouaches for an exhibition in 1973, recalled: 'He didn't want them to become objects of art … What he wanted was the gouache to simply float on the wall.'[9] That said, there is plenty of evidence that Hilton maintained his view of himself

50
Untitled June 1974
1974
Gouache and charcoal on paper 48.3 × 39.4

The British Museum

51
Untitled 1973
Gouache and charcoal on paper 55.9 × 39.4

The British Museum

as a professional artist and of these late works as legitimate product. 'I am doing just as good painting as has been produced', he wrote in one note.[10] It is also clear that he was anxious for opportunities to show the new works and that he was conscious of their value. Right at the beginning of his letter to Townsend he noted, 'Since Dec '72 I have produced 3 to 5 gouaches a day, now valued for a considerable sum'.[11] It has even been suggested that he embarked on this period of extraordinary productivity as a future investment for his family.[12] Less speculatively, his notes record the attention he gave to his materials and their longevity (he is said to have contacted the paint manufacturers to check the pigments would not fade with time): 'I have to have materials not just childrens' stuff. One has to be fair to one's clients', he wrote. Though he did conclude, 'Balls. I am on the last run. It doesn't matter what materials I use.'[13]

It is easy to be distracted by the dramatic change in the physical nature of Hilton's work in his last years and by the circumstances that brought those paintings about. There is also, however, the question of their subject matter. For an artist whose career had been dominated by a continual negotiation between

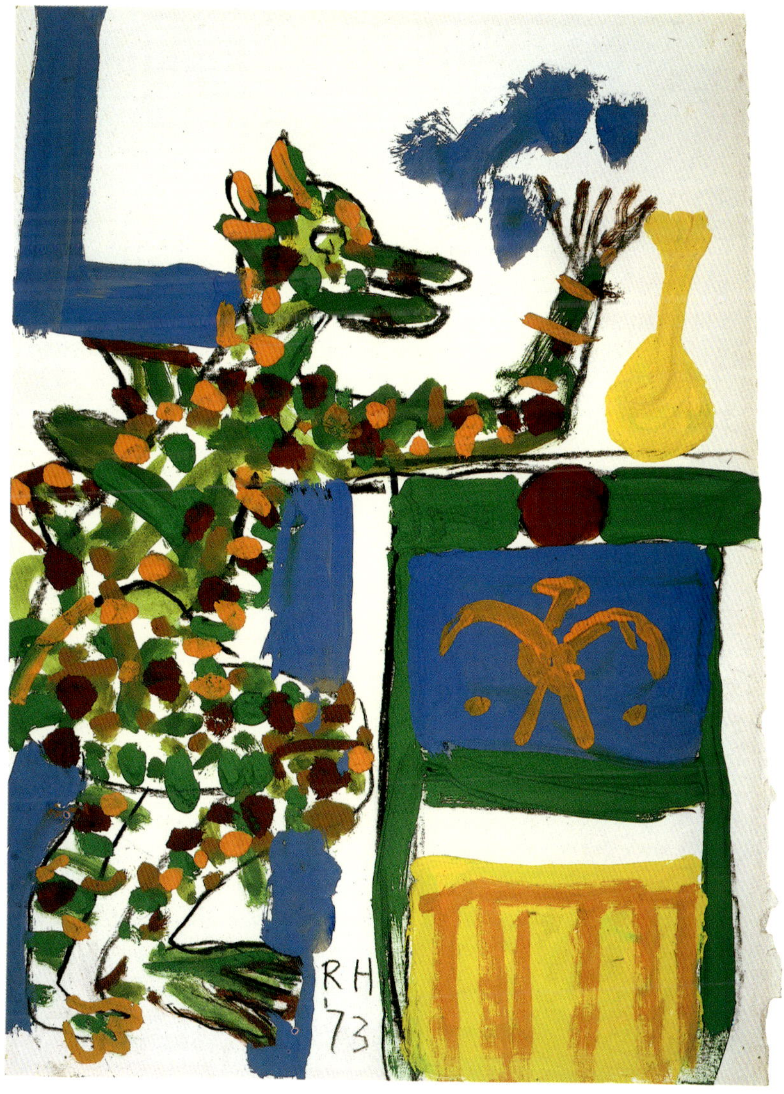

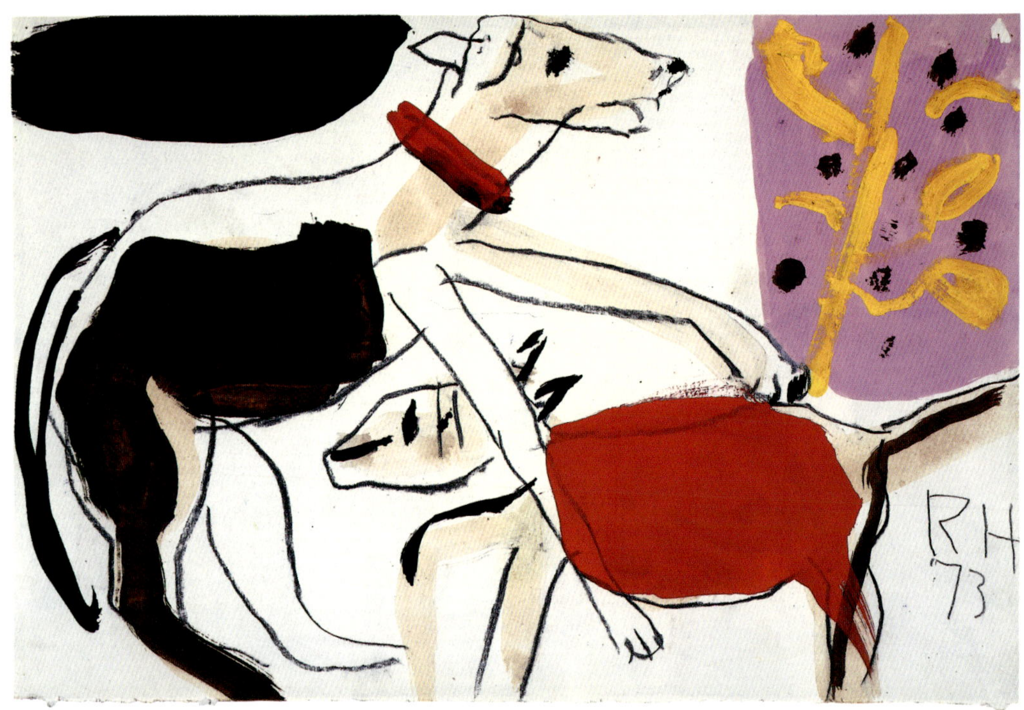

abstraction and figuration, to even talk of subject matter seems to signal a massive departure. As we have seen, the human figure became a much more consistent and overt presence in Hilton's paintings in the 1960s. In these late gouaches, however, its appearance becomes even more consistent and often more specific. On occasion, multi-figure compositions, suggestions of spatial contexts and other paraphernalia even go so far as to allude to specific narratives. As we shall see, these might often be read in terms of Hilton's actual situation or as enactments on paper of conscious or subconscious memories and desires. One wonders if, by extension, such meanings might be read into other works of the period. For instance, it is probably the case that depictions of animals constitute the largest group. Were these simply depictions of creatures, familiar or otherwise, or do they serve a symbolic function also?

The menagerie that Hilton brought to life on paper was as diverse as it was full. Elephants feature strongly, particularly circus elephants, and cats. Dogs are common. Birds appear often, mostly not alone but hovering or swooping over more complex scenes. Cows, horses, bears, spiders, fish, lobsters, camels, butterflies and at least one caterpillar make their appearance. Crocodiles also occur, though in one note the artist observed he could not 'do' crocodiles. In some works, there is simply the single creature and nothing else. In others, it is part of a larger scene or it enacts some absurdly human-like activity. In each, Hilton demonstrates powers of observation and depiction, as the images seem to capture and convey the character of the species. It has been suggested that these animals might also be read as standing for the artist himself, surrogates through which he could express his situation. Though Hilton himself said he resorted to pointillist techniques in order to animate the inert poster paint, others have seen the spotted appearance of some of the animals and figures as denoting the artist's skin complaint. Thus the beast that raises its hand beside a vase (fig.51) is identified as 'a self portrait of the painter reaching for the whisky bottle, the bird

52
Untitled 1973
Gouache and charcoal
on paper 38 × 56
Tate

53
Untitled 1973
Gouache and charcoal
on paper 38.1 × 55.9
The British Museum

taunting him for his immobility'.[14] Similarly, and even more poignantly, in this reading Hilton is the bear who dances with abandon with the ghostly black figure of death (see fig.53).

Personal references are less ambiguously evident in a group of more narrative works, the titles or themes of some of which appear as part of the image. The idea behind a work such as that inscribed *Plan for Extension to Hilton House* (fig.54) seems clear, as it does in the *Revised Plan for Hilton Dwelling*. These works illustrate a point made by David Brown that 'many of the gouaches reflect life around Hilton as he lay in bed'.[15] On one level, such drawings are the sort of thing anyone might make – a visual representation for the greenhouse extension that would improve one's house. Hilton's unmistakeable touch, however, transforms such a mundane sketch into a more eloquent and expressive image. Hilton lived in the room beneath his former studio, somewhat detached from the heart of the house. This unusual arrangement seems to have caused a degree of concern or at least attention as he contemplated how family life may continue with him isolated and ever present. How the set-up might be made to work successfully and how it might be improved to reduce the inconveniences seems to have been a recurring theme. The letter to Townsend demonstrates the way in which the artist saw the intrusion of domestic life as a hindrance to creativity and an inevitability: 'Because he [the artist] has all the usual things to cope with he is not just in an ivory tower. Electrical appliances. Cats drinking his paint water & so on.'

Consciously or unconsciously, escape seems to have occupied Hilton's imagination. Numerous pictures show him with his family on a journey. In one, the bespectacled artist sits behind the wheel of a grand motor car with a luscious-looking group of passengers. In several pictures, he and his family appear in a horse-drawn cart. Sometimes, the cart appears without a horse in what has been read by some as a symbol of impotence or decline. What is, perhaps, both telling

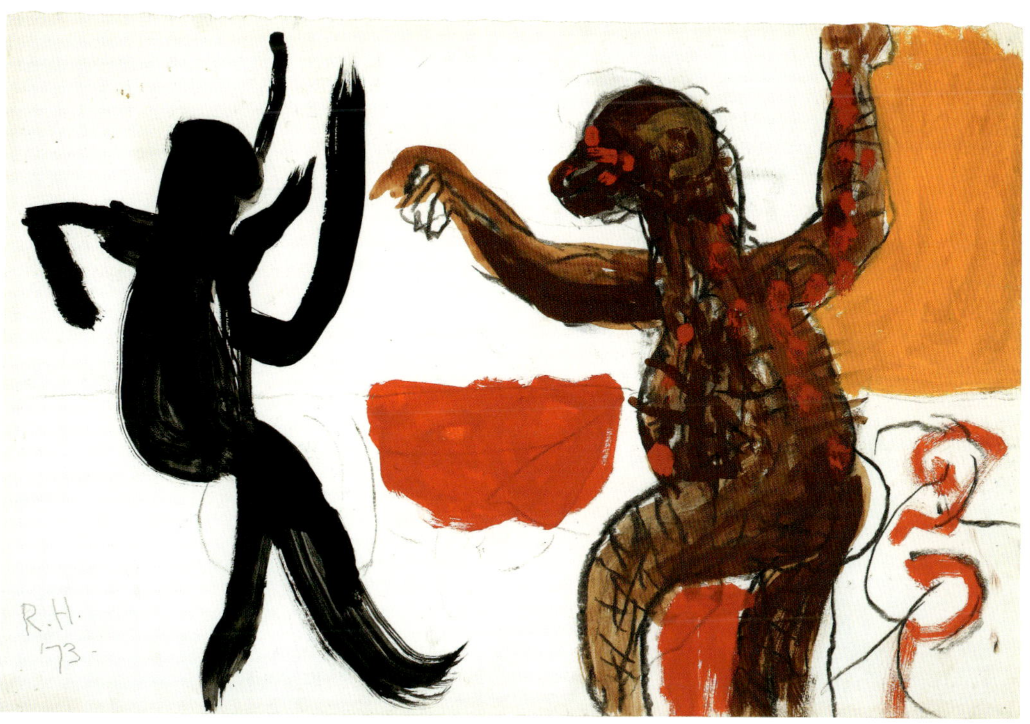

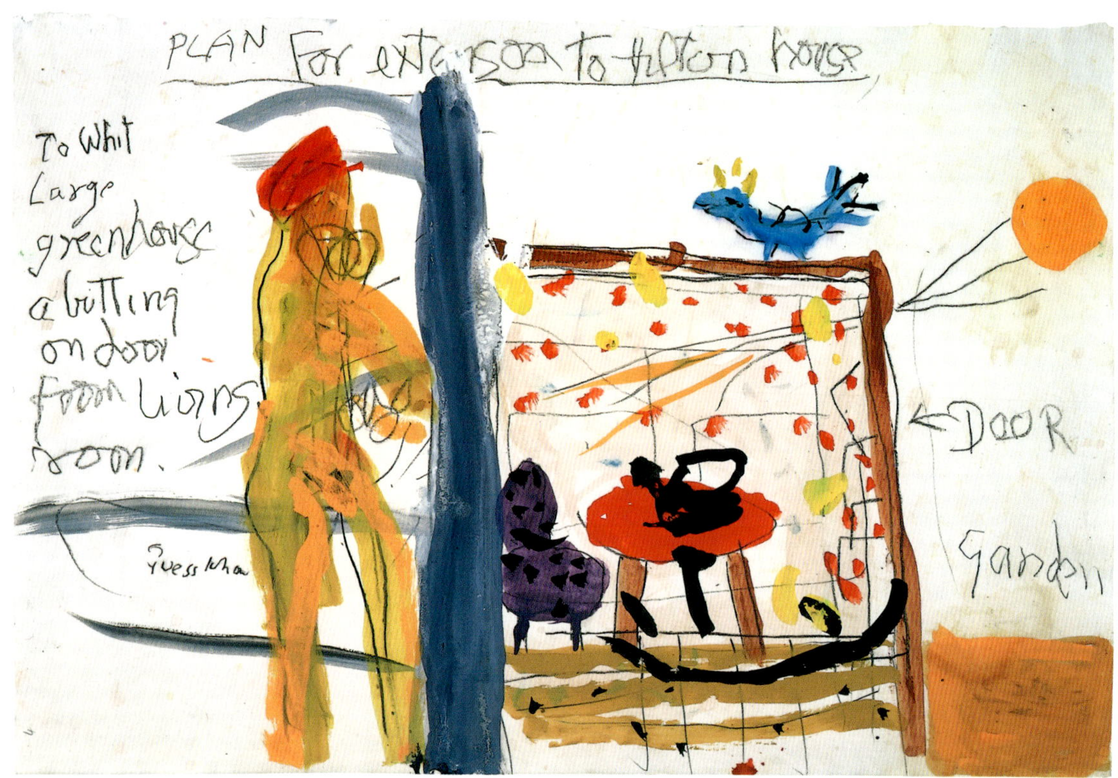

and touching is that the cart of these images frequently resembles a toy from Hilton's childhood that had featured in his youthful paintings and which remained in his possession all his life. Thus they become fantasies of escape into a rural past and, specifically, into the past of the artist's own childhood. It is, in fact, striking that many of the motifs that appear in the late gouaches had been favourite themes of Hilton's childhood drawings: the horse and cart, circus animals and fairgrounds appeared, as did plans of houses, actual or imagined, and aerial views of landscapes. These last might be seen as attempts by the artist to rationalise the world around him or else to weave imaginative worlds according to his own plans. Perhaps one can extend such a reading to the images made late in life of his house and its imagined revisions and extensions.

A third mode of transport that appears repeatedly in the late gouaches is the boat. Of course, in Hilton's earlier painting boat forms had featured and their echoing of breasts and buttocks seemed more than coincidental. Now these boats appeared more literal and often manned. Though some seem to transport groups of people, perhaps the artist and his family, others carry just a single figure. Inevitably, these can seem touching, even a little pathetic, as the solitary seaman might seem to drift or be borne towards his end. The sea was a common symbol of death or the loss of self and had been used as such by several St Ives artists including Hilton's great friend, the poet W.S. Graham, in his long poem *The Nightfishing*. So, such images of solitary sailors might be compared, perhaps, with the bear that dances with the black figure of death. It is clear that Hilton could find different symbolic purposes for the ship, however. In one of the better known of these late images, a sailing ship reminiscent of vessels from childhood pirate stories ploughs through the sea which, on closer examination, is a headless female nude (see fig.55). In this case, then, the ship becomes a phallic symbol of

54
Untitled (Plan for Extension to Hilton House) 1973
Pencil and gouache on paper 76.2 × 101.6
Private Collection

male sexual potency. This apparent paradox of the boat symbolising both an impotent drift towards death and a virile sexual domination is a contradiction that one might find running through Hilton's late works and, perhaps, his last years in general.

At the same time as the late gouaches, Hilton's condition led to the writing of what have become known as his 'Night Letters'. These were a series of manuscript notes written, mostly, for his wife, and often illustrated. As their name (which derives from the title of a posthumous anthology of some of them) indicates, they were often composed at night to be read and acted upon in the morning. They consist of letters, shopping lists or other instructions, and comments and musings on his own condition. At first glance they can seem to reveal Hilton as a demanding and egotistical ogre. On closer reading, however, one discerns a more affectionate, clearly humorous, intelligent and charismatic person. Inevitability, one begins to see a strange combination of tragedy and absurdity in his poignant situation. We see him, like most artists, as a dominating personality but one made impotent by circumstance; a King Lear-like character. Through his forceful personality and demanding nature, communicated by means of these notes, Hilton continued to dominate his household even as he might lie in bed listening to, but cut off from, the life of the rest of the house.

The nocturnal notes also reveal how important fantasy was as a means of escape from current circumstances and, perhaps, a sense of disappointment and loss that they represented. For example, a shopping list might start as a mundane instruction for Rose to go to nearby St Just for basic provisions but gradually develop into a plea for the finest, mostly French, food, itemised as if the note's author were savouring the memory of such tastes. Memory seems a crucial aspect of these fantasy feasts, as if Hilton were recalling a golden age when foie gras were readily available. Adrian Lewis has related this conjuring up of a past idyll in paint and fantasy to Hilton's own description of his pre-war painting as 'a means of attaining … the ideal'.[16] It is not just food that occupied Hilton's thoughts. A similar combination of desire, fantasy and memory for something lost pervades his musings on sex. This is, perhaps, especially illuminating when considering his depictions of eroticised nudes. An 'edgy eroticism', to use a phrase

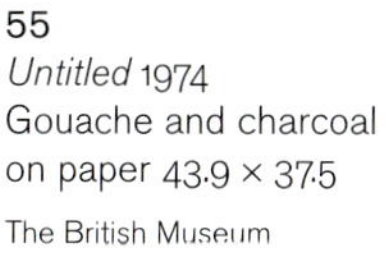

55
Untitled 1974
Gouache and charcoal
on paper 43.9 × 37.5

The British Museum

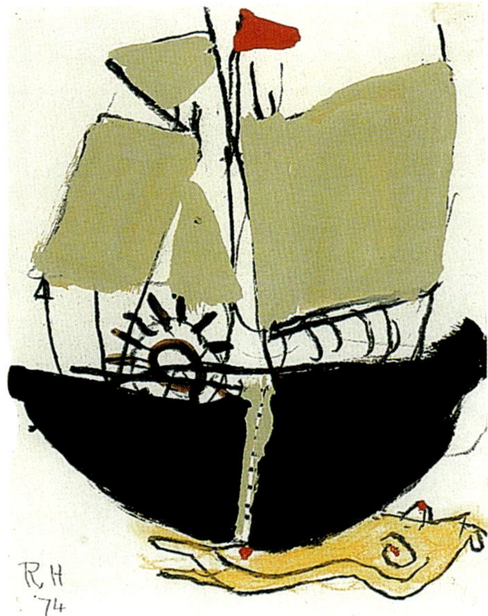

of David Brown's, had long been an aspect of Hilton's work.[17] This continued in the late gouaches where, despite his own warning, the nude remained a favourite theme. One such image (fig.56) is typical: the figure has been drawn with Hilton's distinctive charcoal line − continuous, confident despite the shakiness that crept into the later drawings, and somehow able to suggest the erotic charge of the forms that it describes. The object of the picture is equally bold, her hands on her head opening her body up for the gaze. Finally, an extra erotic charge is injected by the addition of scarlet nipples and a bright blue triangle of pubic hair.

Hilton's intelligence was subtle enough to understand the complex sexual politics that enshroud such an image. The ways in which he depicted the female body seem to signal a conscious demonstration of the fact that such representations are acts of objectification and of domination through the gaze. This, however, would be far too simple an analysis of the complexity of relationships between the artist, the viewer and the image and between the fantasy figure of the picture and actual sexual relationships. This becomes especially clear in Hilton's last years as the letters show how behind these bold depictions of erotic female figures lie the artist's anxieties about his own sexual impotence − as a result of his illness − and of the potential consequences for his wife and their relationship. The 'Night Letters' and related documents and drawings are peppered with references to Hilton's loss of sexual potency. 'It is true,' he told Townsend, 'as my wife points out, that I no longer have any balls.'[18] Several drawings show an erect penis, or a self-portrait with an erection along with an ironic comment. 'I don't think so', he wrote beside one bright red phallus. Hilton's luscious, sexy nudes are fantasies which become charged with an even greater poignancy when one understands this loss of sexuality and the degree of anxiety it must have caused a man for whom a certain kind of masculinity had been so important.

One should be wary of reading works of art as expressions of unconscious desires too deeply or too literally. The apparently impulsive nature of these last works of Hilton's and the nature of his own situation are such that it is hard to resist such a temptation, however. There is one group that seems especially expressive and unsettling. In one the scene is dominated by a series of red forms along the top that may suggest a range of distant hills (see fig.57). Among the other forms and colours of this unusually cluttered scene, in the lower right hand corner, one finds a diminutive red figure, perhaps a child. Something about its isolation and small scale amid its surroundings gives it a pathetic vulnerability and melancholy. In another work, another child-like figure sits disconsolate under a

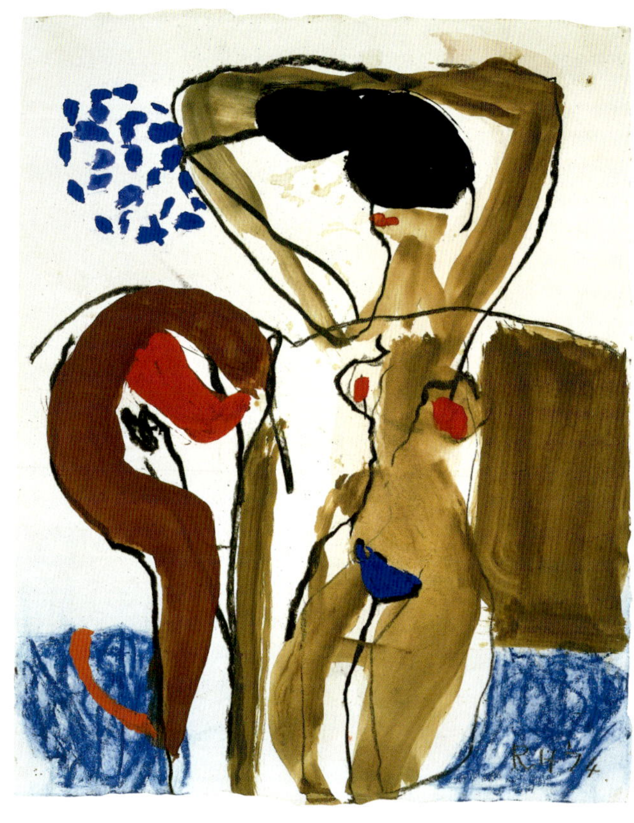

56
Untitled 1974
Pastel, gouache and charcoal on paper
41.9 × 32.4
The British Museum

57
Untitled 1974
Gouache and charcoal on paper 34.3 × 41.3
Private Collection

structure which a jug and pot plant identify unambiguously as a table (see fig.58). Whether, as has been suggested, the triangular form beside the child should be read as a long road heading into the distance, this seems to be an archetypal image of childhood loneliness rendered with an almost unbearable degree of accuracy.[19]

One of Hilton's fantasies was realised when, in August 1974, he chartered a plane from nearby St Just aerodrome and, at one hour's notice, he, Rose and their two sons, with only a carrier bag containing swimming costumes and whisky, embarked on a seven hour flight to Antibes. Though bed-bound since late 1972, Hilton had managed to be at the opening of his major retrospective at London's Serpentine Gallery in March 1974. That his only other venture from his room was to Antibes demonstrates the importance to him of French Mediterranean culture. As if to indicate this, many of the gouaches made on that trip are inscribed 'Antibes'.

The experience of the trip, like these paintings, was all the more intense because of the awareness of the proximity of death. The category of 'late work' is not uncommon in art history, yet it is none the less rare for artists to experience such a late flourish of creativity while aware of their imminent demise. That Hilton was conscious of his situation is demonstrated by one work, which consists simply of the words 'The Last Days of Hilton'.[20] Though less explicit, while the late works possess all the spontaneity and artistic instinct of the earlier oils, it is through their bright palette, rapid marks and witty and sexy subject matter that one can frequently discern the figure of approaching death.

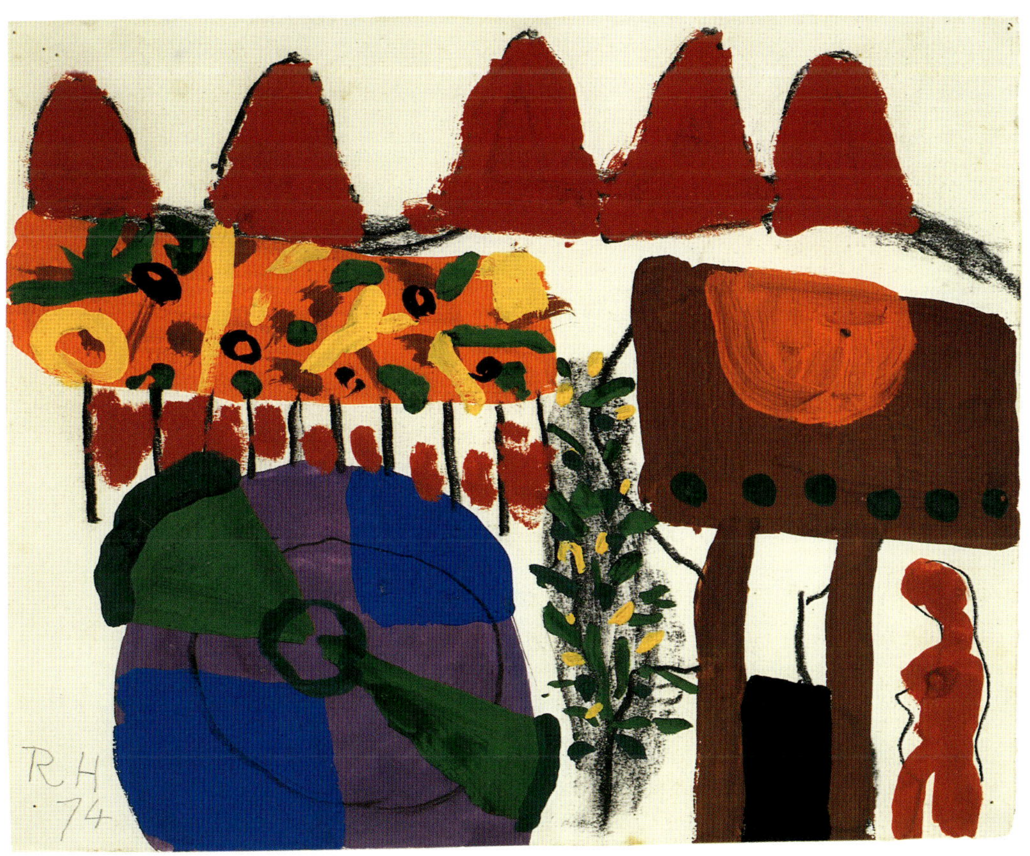

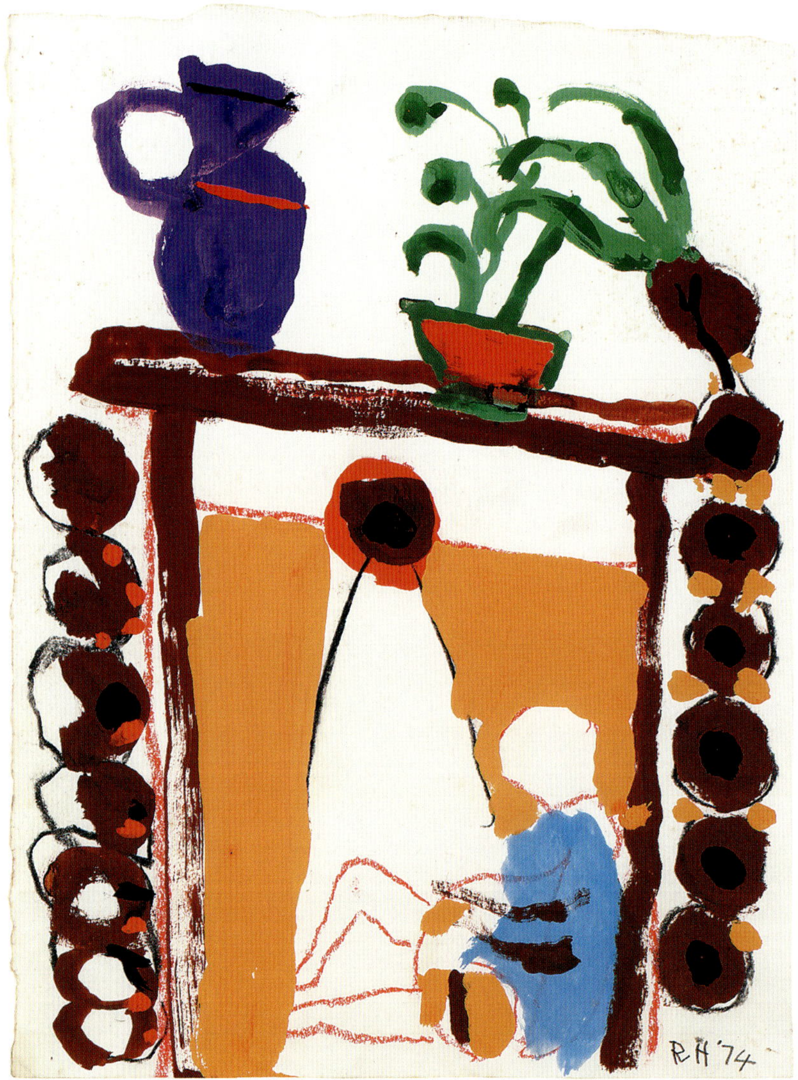

Roger Hilton died following a stroke at home on 23 February 1975. He had declined in his last weeks and, while he continued to work almost to the last, an awareness of his approaching end may be the reason why he, unusually, inscribed the month as well as the year on the last paintings. After his death, under his bed was found a 'night letter' inscribed with the text from the 23rd Psalm, 'Yea though I pass through the valley of death, I fear no evil. Thy rod and thy staff shall comfort me'. The text is followed by a drawing of a sly-looking serpent beneath which sits a buxom nude and the unfinished children's rhyme, 'Adam and Eve and Pinchme went down to the river to bathe'.[21] Solemnity and mischievous humour as part of a broader attitude of defiance, cynical questioning, trouble-making and incisive and ruthless intelligence were vital parts of Hilton's make-up. They are also central to his art.

In the best works of his short career, Hilton combined some of the characteristics of the most important artists of the modern age. He had the innovative defiance and disrespect for orthodoxy of Pollock; the graphic dexterity and edgy eroticism of Picasso and the colour sense and lusciousness of Matisse. Beneath what could seem like a faultless intuition for expressive mark-making lay a sophisticated understanding of where the future of painting lay. Historical and cultural circumstances prevented Hilton from becoming a leading figure in the international history of modernist painting, but time has shown his revision of what painting might be to be more profound and longer lasting than that of many who garnered more glory in their lifetimes.

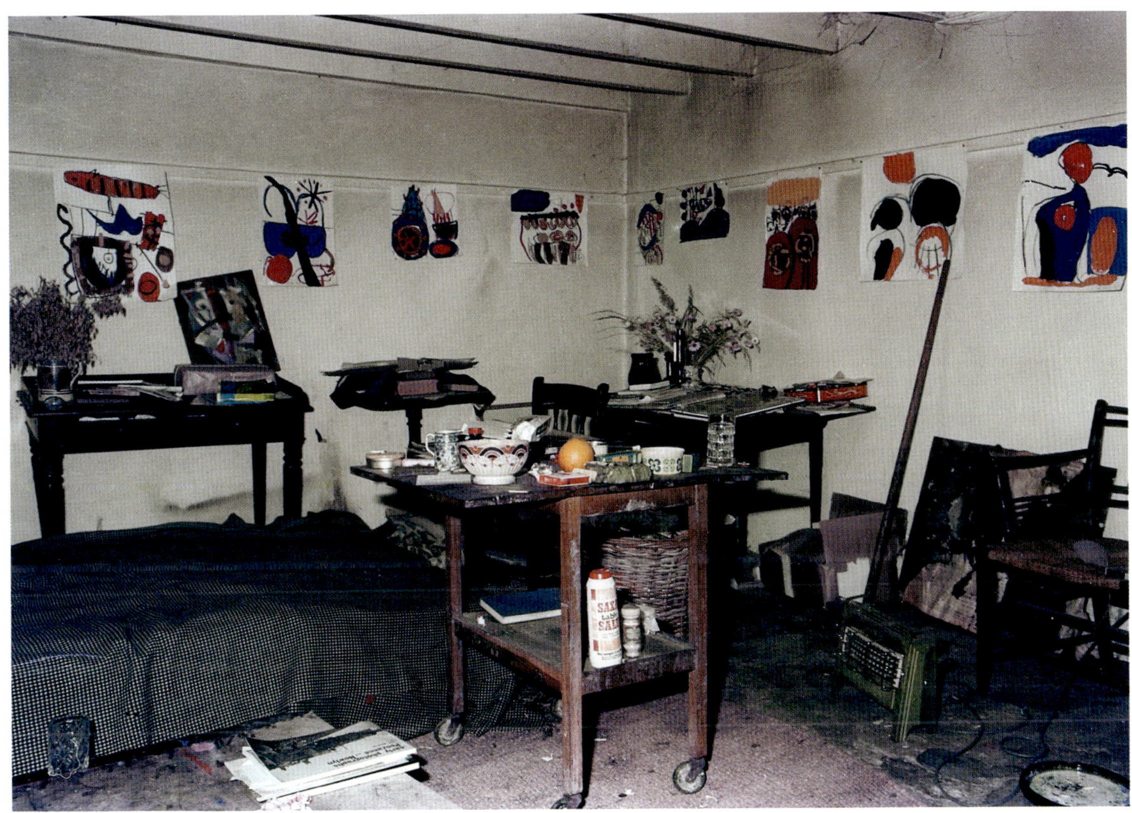

Notes

INTRODUCTION

1 Charles Harrison, 'Roger Hilton: The Obligation to Express', *Roger Hilton*, exh. cat., Hayward Gallery, South Bank Centre, London 1993, p.16.

2 Nick Waterlow in conversation with the author, Sydney, February 2006.

3 Patrick Heron, 'Paintings by Roger Hilton', *New Statesman and Nation*, 28 June 1952, p.771. Reprinted in Patrick Heron, *The Changing Forms of Art*, London 1955, p.200.

4 Roger Hilton, 'Every Artist is a Con-Man' *Studio International*, vol.187, no. 964, March 1974, p.119.

5 Adrian Lewis, 'Roger Hilton and the Culture of Painting', unpublished Ph.D thesis, University of Manchester, 1995; Adrian Lewis, *Roger Hilton*, London 2003.

6 Lawrence Alloway (ed.), *Nine Abstract Artists*, London 1954; typescripts survive of Hilton's original, longer draft: 'Thoughts on Abstract Painting by Roger Hilton', RHA.

7 Roger Hilton, 'writings sheet 12', RHA.

8 John Hilton, 'An Early Roger Hilton (Uncompleted Mosaic)', 1989 memoir printed in Lewis 1995, p.497.

9 Roger Hilton, 'writings sheet 12, entitled "Thoughts on Abstract Painting" (1954)', RHA.

10 Roger Hilton, 'writings sheet 20', RHA.

11 Roger Hilton, letter to Peter Townsend in 'Every Artist is a Con-man', *Studio International*, vol.187, no.964, March 1974, p.120.

12 Roger Hilton, 'writings sheet 9', RHA.

13 Roger Hilton, 'writings sheet 13', RHA.

1 1911–1952

1 Roger Hilton, MS annotations to Alan Bowness, 'A note on the painting of Roger Hilton' in *Roger Hilton*, exh. cat., Galerie Charles Lienhard , Zurich 1961.

2 Louisa Hilton, diary, 7 May 1929 quoted in Adrian Lewis, 'Chronology', in *Roger Hilton: The Early Years 1911–55*, exh. cat., Leicester Polytechnic Gallery, November 1984, p.13.

3 Henry Tonks, MS note to Mrs Green, 29 April 1930, RHA, quoted in Lewis 1984, p.14.

4 Quoted in Lewis 1984, p.15.

5 Peggy Hilton, notes, quoted in Lewis 1984, p.16.

6 Letter to parents postmarked Paris 24 December 1931.

7 Letter to parents postmarked Paris 12 January 1932.

8 See Lewis 1984, p.16 and Hayward Gallery 1993, p.34.

9 Anthony Blunt in the *Spectator*, 31 January 1936, p.171, quoted in Lewis 1984, p.17.

10 Letter to parents postmarked Morecambe 20 May 1942, quoted Lewis 1984, p.21.

11 'Ruth Hilton Memoir' printed in Lewis 1995, pp.481–6, quoted in Lewis 1984, p.22.

12 Roger Hilton, MS notes, c.1961, quoted in Lewis 1995, p.32.

13 Quoted in Lewis 1984, p.21.

14 'Ruth Hilton Memoir', quoted Lewis 1984, p.26.

15 Bernard Denvir in *Art News and Review*, 10 August 1950, quoted in Lewis 1984, p.27.

16 Patrick Heron, 'Five Types of Abstraction: Roger Hilton', in Heron 1955, p.201.

17 Ibid.

18 Alloway 1954, p.10.

19 The latter term was used in association with the exhibition *L'Imaginaire*, Galerie du Luxembourg, Paris 1947; see Fiona Gaskin, 'British Tachisme in the Post-War Period 1946–57', in Margaret Garlake (ed.), *Artists and Patrons in Post-War Britain*, Aldershot 2001, p.46–7.

20 Eric Newton in *Time and Tide*, 28 June 1952, quoted in Lewis 1984, p.28.

21 Patrick Heron, 'Paintings by Roger Hilton', *New Statesman and Nation*, 28 June 1952, p.771. Reprinted in Patrick Heron, *The Changing Forms of Art*, London 1955, p.200.

22 Letter to mother quoted in Lewis 1984, p.29.

23 'Ruth Hilton Memoir', ibid.

2 1953–1954

1 For a comparison of similar works by Hilton, Constant, Gilbert and Poliakoff see Lewis 2003, pp.42–3; Heron cited Poliakoff as the most likely source for this mode of working in 'Five Types of Abstraction: Roger Hilton', in Heron 1955, p.201.

2 Alloway 1954, p.6; Hilton's statement in the same volume, pp.29–30.

3 Roger Hilton, 'writings sheet 12 entitled "Thoughts on Abstract Painting" (1954)', RHA.

4 Hilton interview with Reg Watkiss in Lewis 1995, p.526.

5 Roger Hilton, 'writings sheet 5', RHA.

6 Constant, 'Spatiaal colorisme', published on the occasion of the *Voor een Spatiaal Colorisme* exhibit at the Stedelijk Museum, Amsterdam, 1952.

7 Quoted in Adrian Lewis, 'Chronology', in Hayward Gallery 1993, p.110.

8 Patrick Heron, 'Introducing Roger Hilton', *Arts* (NY), vol.31, no.8, May 1957, reprinted in Mel Gooding (ed.), *Painter as Critic: Patrick Heron, Selected Writings*, Tate Gallery Publishing 1998, p.133; I am grateful to Lynne Green for giving me a preview of her essay 'Peter Stead and the Artists'.

9 Heron 1957/1998, p.133.

10 Charles Harrison, 'Roger Hilton: the Obligation to Express', Hayward Gallery 1993, pp.25–6.

3 1955–1959

1 'Ruth Hilton Memoir' in Lewis 1995, p.484.

2 Lewis 1995 suggests Hilton and Graham met at Christmas in 1956 but it must have been earlier as a manuscript copy of Graham's poem 'Hilton Abstract' is dated 13 November 1956, and the poet wrote on 13 December to thank Hilton for having him to stay in London. See Michael and Margaret Snow (eds.), *The Nightfisherman: Selected Letters of W.S. Graham*, Manchester 1999, pp.153–5.

3 Information from 'Ruth Hilton Memoir' and 'Biographical Events', both in Lewis 1995, and David Brown (ed.), *St Ives: Twenty-Five Years of Painting, Sculpture and Pottery*, exh. cat., Tate Gallery, London 1985, p.127.

4 Letter to Terry Frost, n.d. (?March 1955), Tate Archive (TA) 7919.

5 Letter to Terry Frost, n.d. (but before September 1955), TA 7919.

6 Letter to Terry Frost, n.d. (summer 1955), TA 7919.

7 Letter to Terry Frost, n.d. (summer 1955), TA 7919.

8 Letter to Terry Frost, n.d. (summer 1955) TA 7919.

9 Ibid.

10 Letter to Terry Frost, n.d. (but before September 1955), TA 7919.

11 Letter to Terry Frost, 24 July [1963], TA 7919, published in *Phoebus*, no.1, 1976, pp.68–9.

12 Letter to William Scott, n.d. [1956], William Scott Archive A/10/0040.

13 Patrick Heron, in Heron 1957/1998, writes that the works from 1957 had been made during three months recently spent in St Ives.

14 Letter to William Scott, n.d. [1956], William Scott Archive A/10/0040.

15 Heron 1957/1998, p.134.

16 Roger Hilton, letter to Tate Gallery, n.d. [May 1960] quoted in Mary Chamot, Dennis Farr and Martin Butlin, *Tate Gallery Catalogues: The Modern British Paintings, Drawings and Sculpture* vol.1, London 1964, p.286.

4 1960–1972

1 In conversation with the author c.1990. It should be noted that Frost happily admitted to embellishing his anecdotes.

2 Roger Hilton, MS notes, c.1961, quoted in Lewis 1995, p.32.

3 Roger Hilton, 'Statement', *Roger Hilton: Painting 1953–7*, ICA, London 1958.

4 Ibid.

5 Roger Hilton in Zurich 1961, unpaginated.

6 Letter to Peter Townsend, 1974.

7 Roger Hilton, letters to Clement Greenberg, n.d. and 14 August 1960, Archives of American Art, Smithsonian Institution, Washington D.C. N69-91R and Greenberg's replies, 10 August and 2 September 1960, RHA.

8 Letter to Terry Frost, 24 July [1963].

9 Draft of a letter to Lawrence Alloway (original possibly never sent), 12 October 1957, RHA printed in Lewis 1995, p.520.

10 Letter to Terry Frost, 24 July [1963].

11 Hilton, draft letter to Alloway, 12 October 1957.

12 Pierre Rouve, 'Roger Hilton', *Quadrum*, no.12, 1961, p.92.

13 In Hayward 1993, cat.50.

14 Terry Frost, 'Still crazy after all these years', *Art Line*, vol.4, no.8, autumn 1989, p.19.

15 Letter to Terry Frost, n.d. (1965), TA 7919.

16 Letter to Terry Frost, n.d. [post marked 1965], TA 7919.

17 Norbert Lynton, review in *Studio International*, 1971

5 1972–1975

1 Lewis 1995.

2 Roger Hilton, letter to Peter Townsend, in 'Every Artist is a Con-Man', *Studio International*, vol.187, no.964, March 1974, p.117.

3 Hilton, letter to Peter Townsend 1974.

4 Hilton, letter to Peter Townsend 1974.

5 Hilton, letter to Peter Townsend 1974.

6 Hilton, letter to Peter Townsend 1974.

7 Hilton, letter to Peter Townsend 1974.

8 Alan Bowness in conversation with the author, 17 March 2006.

9 John Miller quoted in Adrian Lewis, *The Last Days of Hilton*, Bristol 1996, p.89.

10 Roger Hilton, MS repr. in Rosemary Hilton (ed.), *Roger Hilton: Night Letters and Selected Drawings*, Newlyn Orion Galleries, Newlyn 1980, unpaginated.

11 Letter to Peter Townsend 1974.

12 Jeremy Le Grice, quoted in Lewis 1990, p.90.

13 Roger Hilton, MS repr. in Rosemary Hilton (ed.), *Roger Hilton: Night Letters and Selected Drawings*, Newlyn Orion Galleries, Newlyn 1980, unpaginated.

14 David Brown, 'Roger Hilton – Late Gouaches', *Roger Hilton: Last Paintings*, exh. cat., Graves Art Gallery, Sheffield, May 1980, p.3.

15 Ibid.

16 Lewis 1996, p.57.

17 David Brown, 'Introduction', *Roger Hilton*, exh. cat., Waddington Galleries, London 1983, p.3.

18 Letter to Townsend.

19 Lewis 1996, p.36.

20 Repr. Lewis 1996, p.1.

21 Repr. in Rosemary Hilton (ed.), unpaginated.

Select Bibliography

Roger Hilton statement in LAWRENCE ALLOWAY (ed.), *Nine Abstract Artists*, London 1954

PATRICK HERON, 'Five Types of Abstraction: Roger Hilton' in *The Changing Forms of Art*, London 1955

PATRICK HERON, 'Introducing Roger Hilton', *Arts* (NY), vol.31, no.8, May 1957, reprinted in MEL GOODING (ed.), *Painter as Critic: Patrick Heron: Selected Writings*, Tate Gallery Publishing 1998

ROGER HILTON, 'Statement' in *Roger Hilton: Paintings 1953–7*, exh. cat., Institute for Contemporary Arts, London 1958

NORBERT LYNTON, 'The Englishness of Roger Hilton', *Art News and Review*, 7–21 May 1960, pp.15–7

ROGER HILTON, 'Remarks about Painting' in *Roger Hilton*, exh. cat., Galerie Charles Lienhard, Zurich 1961

ALAN BOWNESS, 'Introduction' in *Roger Hilton*, exh. cat., Galerie Charles Lienhard, Zurich 1961

ROGER HILTON, letter to Peter Townsend and 'Every Artist is a Con-Man: interview with Alan Green' in *Studio International*, vol.187, no.964, March 1974, pp.117–21

ROSEMARY HILTON (ed.), *Roger Hilton: Night Letters and Selected Drawings*, Newlyn Orion Gallery, Newlyn 1980

ADRIAN LEWIS, *Roger Hilton: The Early Years 1911–55*, exh. cat., Leicester Polytechnic Gallery, Leicester 1984

DAVID BROWN (ed.), *St Ives: Twenty-Five Years of Painting, Sculpture and Pottery*, exh. cat., Tate Gallery, London 1985

MARTIN CAIGER-SMITH (ed.), *Roger Hilton*, exh. cat., Hayward Gallery, London 1993

ADRIAN LEWIS, 'Roger Hilton and the Culture of Painting', unpublished Ph.D thesis, University of Manchester 1995

ADRIAN LEWIS, *The Last Days of Hilton*, Bristol 1996

ADRIAN LEWIS, *Roger Hilton*, Aldershot 2003

Photographic Credits & Copyright

Index